THE MASTER PLAN

RETIREMENT STRATEGIES FOR THE BEST OF YOUR LIFE

THE MASTER PLAN

RETIREMENT STRATEGIES FOR THE BEST OF YOUR LIFE

JEFF TOWNSEND

THE PUBLISHING COOPERATIVE
Denver

THE PUBLISHING COOPERATIVE
1836 Blake St.
Denver, CO 80202
mailroom@penclay.com

Publishing Cooperative books are available at special discounts for reprint editions, bulk purchases, sales promotions, fund raising and educational purchases. Contact: Sales Department, The Publishing Cooperative, Finance Station, P.O. Box 480151, Denver, CO 80202; salesdepartment@penclay.com

Library of Congress Cataloging-in-Publication Data

Townsend, Jeff, 1958 -
The master plan : retirement strategies for the best of your life / .-- 1st ed.
p. cm.
Includes bibliographical references and index.
ISBN 0-9644849-3-5(pbk. : alk. paper)
1. Retirement--United States--Planning. 2. Retirement income. I. Title.

HQ1063.2.U6 T68 2000
646.7'9--dc21

00-062634
CIP

First Edition
10 9 8 7 6 5 4 3 2 1

Printed in the United States of America

Cover design by Ellen Riendeau
Interior illustration by Jim Marr

The paper in this book meets the guidelines for permanence and durability of the Committee on Production Guidelines for Book Longevity of the Council on Library Resources.

∞

Printed on Recycled Paper

To the wonderful girls in my life—Cayle, Emma and Nellie

Contents

Acknowledgments

There are many who helped me write this book in one way or another, and who have helped me get to the place I am today—too numerous to list here, in fact. I would, however, like to mention a few who have been most helpful and understanding.

First and foremost, my career of 16 years would not have been possible had it not been for the wisdom and patience of my beautiful wife Cayle and two lovely children, Nellie and Emma. My work demands 60-70 hours of my life each week; I'm blessed with a very understanding family.

A great big thank you also goes to my staff: Terri Clapper, Sharon Evans, Mark Fuller, Lina Jackson, Jeff Robbins, and Dawn Shellberg. They have made my life easier this past year so that I could find the time to complete *The Master Plan*.

I'd also like to thank my high school buddy Allen Bailey's dad, Richard. Richard Bailey was a New York Life agent who gave me my first exposure to the industry. Also, I'd like to thank my first boss in this industry, Fred Lehrer. An inspirational mentor, Fred was always ready with a quote or saying—many of which have stuck with me to this day. ("If it is to be, it is up to me," and "People do things for *their* reason; not for yours or mine.")

I'd also like to thank the staff of The Publishing Cooperative and, in particular, my editor, Kendall Bohannon—without whom this book would not have been written.

And last—but certainly not least—a very heartfelt thank you to my clients who have entrusted their life savings and their hopes and dreams to my firm. If not for them, there would be neither a book nor Townsend and Associates, Inc.

INTRODUCTION

The future ain't what it used to be.

—Yogi Berra

Financial planning is as old as time itself. No doubt the first cave men and women discovered that, in their golden years, killing a saber tooth tiger for dinner (and to trade for spears and clubs and loincloths) wasn't nearly so easy as it was when they were younger. Of course, when they were in their prime, they could spring upon a meal with remarkable agility and, along with their equally agile comrades, clobber the unwitting beast into a feast for many.

Consequently, these very first visionary financial planners no doubt decided to gather nuts and berries and such—none of which would spoil with the passage of time—and store them away for when the aches and pains made hunting the great saber tooth tiger a difficult, if not dangerous, proposition. This, of course, was not so much the result of any diminishment of skills or physical prowess. No, their planning skills were born of wisdom—knowledge gathered and processed, then applied to life according to the lessons of experience—something those

Old age is the most unexpected of all things that happen to a man.

—Leon Trotsky

young warrior studs in their tribe would have to learn for themselves over time.

Now, at the dawn of the 21st century—and after several great leaps forward from our humble origins—Homo sapien has become infinitely more sophisticated, but faces the same challenge: to prepare for the years when the aches and pains keep him from hunting and gathering as enthusiastically as he did when he was younger. And he must do so in a time of great economic uncertainty. For he and his colleagues and peers are on the threshold of a socio-economic shift such as the world has never before seen. Ironically, this is a turn of events that he himself is responsible for in that he and his much heralded Baby Boomer colleagues (and to a certain extent, his Eisenhower-generation parents) were the heart and soul of the greatest period of economic productivity in human history.

DID I EVER TELL YOU ABOUT THE TIME I RAN THE FASTED MILE EVER IN THE HISTORY OF POSSUM CREEK HIGH....

These are the voyages of the Starship Enterprise. It's five-year mission...to boldly go where no man has gone before.

—Gene Roddenberry

Indeed, Baby Boomers (born between 1946 and 1964) constitute the largest generation in the history of the United States. They are the generation that built the most affluent, powerful kingdom the world has ever known. Now they are faced with the challenge of reaping what they have sewn in order to plan for their retirement—an inevitable turn of events that threatens to crumble the very foundation of the magnificent kingdom they built. For when they began building this magnificent kingdom, there were 40 workers per each retiree contributing to Social Security, that sacred institution designed to protect our citizens from the often harsh realities of socio-cultural and economic growth; at the turn of the century, there were about three workers for each retiree. The greatest question mark in the future of our remarkable country is whether there will be funds available to them for their imminent mass exodus from the workforce—the promise our society made to them when they started working.

Consequently, it may be more than just a good idea to plan for retirement above and beyond that which Social Security promises; it may be absolutely necessary. For we are all on the brink of the most dramatic economic change in the history of the magnificent kingdom that Baby Boomers built. As more and more jobs are moving overseas and more and more Baby Boomers retire, there will be fewer and fewer workers paying into the Social Security fund, and more and more Americans who are financially insecure. And the world in which this most accomplished incarnation of Homo sapien faces the monumental challenge of planning for his increasingly insecure retirement is every bit the jungle it was when his intrepid journey began many millennia ago.

Corporate mergers and takeovers can turn fortunes into debt overnight. Inflation can turn life-savings into petty cash. Volatile stock markets in the throes of wild technology speculation can turn mom and pops into Fortune 500s and blue chips into dinosaurs in a single day of trading. Unpredictable interest rates, confusing and ever-changing tax laws, ever-greedy insurance companies,

Let Wall Street have a nightmare and the whole country has to help get them back in bed again.

—Will Rogers

When the politicians complain that TV turns their proceedings into a circus, it should be made plain that the circus was already there, and that TV has merely demonstrated that not all the performers are well trained.

—Edward R. Murrow

Advertising is the rattling of a stick inside a swill bucket.

—George Orwell

mismanaged public trusts (Social Security) and public health programs (Medicare), election-time political proposals designed with little more in mind than getting votes, irresponsible special interest-driven public policy and thoughtless corporate-sponsored legislation, fly-by-night financial advisors who espouse every financial gimmick and speculative opportunity that gets a headline as a magical door to financial independence—all are real and potentially real financial predators, preying on the uninformed and misinformed, hiding in the bushes and behind trees and around every corner. Indeed, the jungle that Homo sapien must survive in now is perhaps even more treacherous than the jungle he maneuvered when first he left the trees for the grassy plains and more abundant food supplies to satisfy his biological imperative. For now the jungle is teeming with vicious lawyers trying to satisfy their sociological imperative: money.

Albert Einstein, that most respected and revered pioneer of the future and *Time* magazine's Man of the 20th Century, had this to say about man's intrepid journey:

> ...the present manifestations of decadence are explained by the fact that economic and technologic developments have highly intensified the struggle for existence, greatly to the detriment of the free development of the individual. But the development of technology means less and less work is needed from the individual for the satisfaction of the community's needs....
>
> This security and the spare time and energy which the individual will have at his disposal can be turned to the development of his personality. In this way the community may regain its health, and we will hope that future historians will

> explain the morbid symptoms of present-day society as the childhood ailments of an aspiring humanity, due entirely to the excessive speed at which civilization was advancing....

Humanity is just a work in progress.

—Tennessee Williams

Always ahead of his time in both matters of science and social philosophy, Einstein wrote his observation on "Society and Personality" in 1934 (*Mein Weltbild*).

RELATIVELY SPEAKING, AS A SOCIETY WE'RE PROBABLY STILL IN OUR TEENS....

Knowledge itself is power.

—Francis Bacon

There are literally thousands of methods and programs intended to make preparing for retirement a snap. It's no small chore to sift through what's out there to find reliable information and/or sound financial planning advice. Our economy, like life itself, is in a state of constant action and reaction, vision and revision.

In the chapters that follow, I will address the issues that face retirees now and in the near future. More important than simply addressing the issues that retirees face, however, I will propose a way of looking at the financial planning landscape that, hopefully, will provide the perspective necessary to see the big picture—what I like to call The Master Plan. Armed with just such a Master Plan that not only informs, but organizes the options and variables

The road of excess leads to the palace of wisdom.

—William Blake

involved in planning for your retirement, my hope is that you'll be able to more effectively chart and navigate your course through the financial planning jungle to that most elusive of human goals: the sacred temple of financial independence.

I find the great thing in this world is not so much where we stand, as in what direction we are moving: To reach the port of heaven, we must sail sometimes with the wind and sometimes against it—but we must sail, and not drift, nor lie at anchor.

—Oliver Wendell Holmes, Sr.

PROLOGUE

THE BALLAD OF BILL AND BETTY BOOMER...

Bill Boomer was born in the summer of 1946. His father had returned home from the war a year earlier and, like so many returning war veterans, had begun his family immediately. By the time Bill was three years old, he already had both a younger brother and sister.

Bill was a precocious child but got good grades. He also excelled at sports. In fact, in high school he was an all-conference tailback—the pride of Mountain View High. His long-time sweetheart Betty was homecoming queen and the prettiest girl in the county—maybe the whole state. After graduation, the rumors and gossip that had been floating around in the barber and beauty shops since their sophmore year were confirmed: In June they became Bill and Betty Boomer and began the fairy tale life they'd always dreamed they'd live.

They enrolled at State where Bill had received a football scholarship. Bill wanted to be an architect and Betty wanted to be a teacher. Bill blew out his knee in the first game of the year, however, and it was unlikely that he'd ever play again. Betty dropped out of school to work full-time so Bill could stay in school and study architecture. She would go back and get her teaching degree after Bill graduated and got a job. A month later, however, she was pregnant, and on Memorial Day 1966, Bill and Betty Boomer gave birth to a nine-pound-one-ounce bouncing baby boy—Bill, Jr.

Of course there was neither the time nor money for either one to continue their education now that they had a child, so Bill, Sr. dropped out of college and got a job with a construction company while Betty stayed home and raised Bill, Jr.

It was a wonderful time for not only them, but for the rest of the country, as well. The United States was in the midst of an unprecedented boom—both in terms of economics and in social development. The country was in a dynamic phase of growth, both in terms of population and affluence. Hollywood and Madison Avenue were forging bonds that would propel the new youth culture to dizzying heights and unprecedented levels of financial success. Consumerism was evolving into a science that would fill business schools for the next half century; the computer age was being born and economic opportunism and speculation was awakening with a promise and potential that had not been seen since the roaring 20s.

Bill's first construction job was on a crew that was putting the finishing touches on the St. Louis Arch. His father's first construction job had been on a crew that built the Golden Gate Bridge. Now Bill understood the pride his father felt—and was never at a loss to remind him about—at having participated in something so magnificent. His father had died while Bill was in high school, and Bill had never fully appreciated what pride in his work meant to his father. Standing underneath the completed arch holding his new baby in the summer of 1966, Bill understood exactly what it meant.

Life was good for the Boomers'—if not for the rest of the country. There was a war in Viet Nam, rioting in the streets at home, violence on campuses all across the country—for that matter, all over the world. It seemed as though someone had flipped a switch and the world had gone crazy. It was into just such an uncertain world that Nellie was born. And the Boomers couldn't have been happier.

Though she never complained, Betty's work seemed never-ending. She made sure Bill, Jr. and Nellie always had clean clothes to wear and Bill, Sr. a hot meal on the table when he got home from work. There was grocery shopping, house-cleaning, bathing the kids and dozens of other thankless jobs that nobody ever noticed. Of course there was a time when she wanted to be a teacher, but this is what she really wanted. And though she knew that, from time to time, Bill, Sr. still thought about how their lives might have been different had he become an architect, she knew that he too wouldn't trade the life they had for anything in the world. And while there were times when they struggled to pay bills on time, buy food and clothing, and have enough left over to put into a savings account for the kids' college education, they were never short on love. Together they built and maintained a happy home and healthy family. There was no doubt in their minds that they'd made the right decisions in life....

CHAPTER ONE

THE WISDOM OF THE AGES

We must consider that we shall be a city upon a hill, the eyes of all the people are on us; so that if we shall deal falsely with our God in this work we have undertaken, and so cause Him to withdraw His present help from us, we shall be made a story and a byword through the world.

—John Winthrop

"For one generation," according to historian Paul Carter, "the population of the United States was expanding at a rate comparable to India's."

Of course the noted historian was speaking of the Baby Boom generation—that much heralded and praised generation of movers and shakers born between 1946 and 1964. It is the same near-mythical generation whose parents fought World War II, who established the United Nations, who built and used the first atomic bomb, and perhaps even more important, who were the most prolific baby-makers in the history of the United States. For when American troops came home triumphantly from fighting Nazi aggression and Japanese imperialism in 1944 and 1945, they were responsible for the largest population explosion in the history of this country. In 1946, 3.4 million babies were born in the U.S.—a 20 percent increase from the year before. And they kept giving birth. By 1957, Eisenhower generation parents were giving birth to 4.3

million babies per year. After 1964, the number of babies born each year began to taper off considerably.

Why should this be important to anyone thinking about planning financially for their retirement? Because the first of this amazing generation will begin retiring in 2011, and there is an alarm as loud as a nuclear explosion going off in the ears of economists and politicians across the country. How will our near-crippled Social Security system make good on the promise it made to them when they entered the workforce?

I pledge you, I pledge myself, to a new deal for the American people.

—Franklin D. Roosevelt

When the first of the Baby Boomers were born, there were nearly 40 workers contributing into each retiree's retirement fund (Social Security). Now there are three. When the first Baby Boomers begin retiring, there could be as few as one worker for each retiree. Baby Boomers, it seems, were not nearly so prolific at making babies as their parents. (And if the manufacturing base continues to erode, like many economists say that it will, and jobs that were once American are moved to China and Mexico and other countries were labor and resources are cheaper, there could be even fewer than one worker per each retiree.)

Children have never been very good at listening to their elders, but they have never failed to imitate them.

—James Baldwin

Perhaps even more disturbing, however, is the fact that it has become very clear in recent years that the children the Baby Boomers did have are not nearly so willing to have money taken out of their paychecks as their parents. Not only haven't Baby Boomers had enough children to insure their retirement, but apparently they've taught the children they have had that the government should keep its paws off their hard-earned money. It is perhaps an unfortunate example of how an admirable—if not short sighted—ethic that Baby Boomers have passed on to their children may very well haunt them in their golden years.

Since the financial plans we make now will be dramatically affected by how we as a country deal with this impending potential economic disaster, the Baby Boomer phenomenon—both the population explosion and the aging of that population—is worth a closer look.

Society is indeed a contract...it becomes a partnership not only between those who are living, but between those who are living, those who are dead, and those who are to be born.

—Edmund Burke

The Population Explosion

In 1946, Dr. Benjamin Spock's magnum opus and revolutionary child care manifesto *Baby and Child Care* was published, proving that even in the grand old pioneering days of American consumerism, commerce was right on top of the latest trends. That phenomenal year saw a birth rate increase of 20 percent from the previous year. In fact, the American population had grown progressively older for 130 years. The median age of Americans had risen every year since 1820—the first year the U.S. had reliable statistics—when it was 16.7 years old. By 1950, it had reached thirty. Then the affect of the Baby Boomers began to be felt, and for the next two decades there was a downward trend in the median age.

As an illustration of just how rapidly the population grew (and America's youth culture developed), consider this: in 1950, there were 776 Little Leagues around the country. Just ten years later in 1960, there were 5,700. During that period of unprecedented growth, a consumer youth culture was born to accommodate the coming-of-age Baby Boomers that changed the course of human history. From mass market advertising and television game shows to Chuck Berry, Elvis and rock and roll, to James Dean, Marilyn Monroe and Hollywood heroes, the consumer youth culture that blossomed organized the American personality into a confident, craving, consuming mass poised to drive the most potent economy in the history of the world.

Baby Boomers sought validation in and with groups, aligning and identifying themselves with their peers and

To found a great empire for the sole purpose of raising up a people of customers, may at first sight appear a project fit only for a nation of shopkeepers. It is, however, a project altogether unfit for a nation of shopkeepers; but extremely fit for a nation whose government is influenced by shopkeepers.

—Adam Smith

Corporations have neither bodies to be punished, nor souls to be condemned, they therefore do as they like.

—Lord Thurlow

institutions that cultivated and fostered the same ideals. They were trained in groups, worked in those same groups, and lived in groups of like-minded, socio-economically and culturally similar people. Suburban communities like Levittown on New York's Long Island sprang up all over the country as Eisenhower-generation G.I.s returned home from the war. The government facilitated this phenomenon (and its own future) by offering them low interest loans and social benefits, which not only reinforced group sensibilities and ideals, but a not-so-quaint idea of American (if not outright divine) providential economic success. This social policy not only insured that the fledgling Baby Boomer generation would be comfortably homogenous in their affluence, but made sure Baby Boomer appetites were whetted for an even bigger slice of the American Dream. Thus was born the philosophy of "Keeping up with the Jones'."

Demographic profiling, long a mainstay of sociologists' laboratories, became the secret weapon of consumer economics, and the modus operandi of government. There is strength and power in numbers, and the job of Madison Avenue and Capitol Hill was to find out the specifics of those numbers—where they lived, how they lived, what they liked, what they disliked, what they believed in, what they didn't believe in, what they dreamed of, what they worried about, what they wanted and what they needed. Thus identified, the mechanism of capitalism (consumerism), and the manifestation of democracy (pop culture) began the task of molding and shaping popular social philosophy and consequently, social norms. The result was an across-the-board hyper-accelerated economic version of the quintessential 19th century American ideal of manifest destiny that affected virtually every aspect and area of American culture.

Fortified by such early profound social and economic success, Baby Boomers came of age without the weighty baggage and intense emotional reminders of war, depression and poverty that had presided over their parents world. As a result, as they began to enter productive society, they tended to shun old values and oppressive, inhibited religious philosophies—the hallmarks of their parents experience—and instead looked to their peers for moral and ethical validation. They had seen the world that these ideals had created—a world at war, bleeding from racism and bigotry, suffering from poverty and hunger. It was a new world, now. And it was crying out for a new approach.

THERE'S NO DOUBT ABOUT IT: WE CHANGED THE WORLD BACK THEN. LATELY IT SEEMS LIKE IT'S CHANGING BACK, THOUGH.

As the Eisenhower generation and their Baby Boomer children began to drive the prototype capitalist economy with its high-powered consumer culture engine, the effects of the sudden and dynamic change in the social and economic fabric began to emerge. With economic prosperity came an enormous amount of leisure time and disposable income with which to pursue leisure activities and buy

The growth of a large business is merely a survival of the fittest... The American beauty rose can be produced in the splendor and fragrance which bring cheer to its beholder only by sacrificing the early buds which grow up around it.

—John D. Rockefeller

The public be damned! I'm working for my stockholders.

—William Vanderbilt

In the factory we make cosmetics; in the store we sell hope.

—Charles Revson

leisure items. Of course consumerism targeted the ever-growing middle class who were the primary beneficiaries of the new American way of life, and our economic system became ever more self-perpetuating.

IT'S SUPPOSED TO BE THE NEXT BIG THING
—YOU KNOW, LIKE 8-TRACKS USED TO BE.

As advertising blather becomes the nation's normal idiom, language becomes printed noise.

—George F. Will

As this remote control effect began to establish itself more and more and the ideals that had created the most successful socio-economic system in the history of the world began to become institutionalized not only in our economic system, but in our political process and collective psyche as well, we began to see social problems that were part and parcel to our success. These problems were unique because no other culture had ever climbed to such dizzying heights of productivity (save Nazi Germany) and prosperity (save the Roman empire) and, for the most part, had never before reared their ugly heads—at least not on the scale that it did during the last half of the 20th century when many Americans thought the world was coming to an end (and indeed, in October of 1962, it appeared as if it just might).

The growing pains of this remarkable generation were considerable (the 60s scared many Americans to death). When the umbilical chord was finally clipped, however, the result was the largest and most affluent generation of humans the world has ever known. With such a large pool of affluence seeking a destiny of its own making within the auspices of a society and culture seemingly created just for them, it is not difficult to see the attraction that Baby Boomers' held for the movers and shakers of the American Dream.

In the 60s, *Time* magazine made Baby Boomers their "Man of the Year" because their buying power determined what was "in" for the whole culture.

It was also in the 60s that the many of the emerging (and in some cases fully grown) youth culture born of this incredible prosperity began to rebel against what it saw as the hypocrisy, short-sighted tunnel vision and lack of understanding of the system that its Eisenhower generation parents had created. They began to question the wisdom and motivation of a war half way around the world in a country that most Americans had never heard of and that few saw any valid reason for fighting.

The youth culture rebelled against the increasingly iron-fisted rule that it believed the military industrial complex was exercising. This idealistic youth culture saw its heroes assassinated and its fellow activists beaten by police on our own streets. The 60s was a time of passionate protest and passionate crack downs as the establishment sought to restore order in what was increasingly seen as an out of control society. The result was violence that threatened to devour both the promise and potential of the tentative republic that, only a decade before, had seemed like the hope of the world.

For every action there is an equal and opposite reaction. The reaction to this social upheaval was an executive branch that began to usurp its role and, in the process,

It is not necessary to advertise food to hungry people, fuel to cold people, or houses to the homeless.

—John Kenneth Galbraith

When the President does it, that means that it is not illegal.

—Richard Nixon

The chief business of the American people is business.

—Calvin Coolidge

All ambitions are lawful except those which climb upwards on the miseries or credulities of mankind.

—Joseph Conrad

For years I thought what was good for our country was good for General Motors and vice versa.

—Charles E. Wilson

destroy the trust and confidence with which Americans had entrusted their government. Nixon's abuse of the office of the president was, in no uncertain terms, an effort to squelch what he saw as a youth culture that lacked respect for the venerable institutions of the country and a political process that had succumbed to this newly empowered youth culture. In many ways, we are still feeling the effects of the suspicion and mistrust of the Nixon administration.

At any rate, the exhaust from the shiny new racing car that our culture had not only invented, but was driving way over the speed limit, was beginning to be felt in a big way. There was a general dissatisfaction with our foreign policy. Most Americans had by now decided that the role of policeman-of-the-world that the Marshall Plan provided for was a mistake, and would result in a country perpetually fighting somebody's else's war.

Moreover, poor planning and foolish management resulted in a disabling energy crisis that exposed the vulnerabilities of America for all the world to see—and take advantage of—and a recession that threatened to garage the shiny high performance American race car indefinitely. Always intimately involved in politics, big business began to blatantly hijack the political process. And there were (and still are, for that matter) plenty of politicians who were eager to please so as to insure their political futures with contributions from the deep pockets of big business. The American political process became a vehicle for supporting the capitalist agenda of the wealthy and connected at all costs. Vast sums of money was spent in order to sell policies to the public and buy politicians who would support those policies with their vote. Thus began the mass market campaign for the soul of the American way of life. Baby Boomers were caught in the crossfire they created.

Tax cuts and other quick-fix vote-getting strategies became the tool big business and its political allies used to put themselves in position to pursue their irresponsible agendas. Throughout the 80s, tax cuts, welfare reform and downsizing government became the battle cry and the social policy that would heal the woes that had garaged the high performance American race car. Ironically, many Baby Boomers were amongst the most ardent supporters of this ideal. Not only did this seem to touch a quintessentially American ideal that government should keep its hands of Americans' hard-earned money, but it also touched that part of the American psyche that was still suspicious of government from the Nixon years. Indeed, economic growth and the creation of wealth became the cure for all social ills during the years of Reaganomics.

You can tell a lot about a fellow's character by his way of eating jelly-beans.

—Ronald Reagan

We used to build civilizations; now we build shopping malls.

—Bill Bryson

I'M NOT SURE I UNDERSTOOD THE SIGNIFICANCE OF WHAT WE WERE REFORMING BACK IN THE 80s. BUT IT SURE SEEMED LIKE A GOOD IDEA AT THE TIME.

Every positive value has its price in negative terms... The genius of Einstein leads to Hiroshima.

—Pablo Picasso

In a comment strangely indicative of the mood and mentality during the 80s, former President Ronald Reagan, in a now infamous blooper, was joking around while waiting for his weekly radio address to the country to start. Under

Nothing is illegal if one hundred well-placed business men decide to do it.

—Andrew Young

He that will not apply new remedies must expect new evils; for time is the greatest innovator.

—Francis Bacon

the impression that the sound was off, he jokingly interviewed himself regarding the then-Soviet Union, whereupon he flippantly said: "We will begin bombing the sons-of-bitches in 30 seconds."

When informed that he was speaking into an open microphone, he tried to cover himself.

"To repeat, I said, 'We're all happy and we're all rich.'"

Apparently during the 80s, many Baby Boomers still thought they would stay young forever, and the socio-political climate they existed in was more than willing to let them think that in order that their economic agenda might be furthered. Unfortunately, it wasn't until the 90s that many of us began to see the storm on the horizon—namely, the exodus of the Baby Boomers from the work-force. Of course by then, the American economic imperative was thoroughly imbedded in the American collective psyche and, while a few responsible members of our society began to scream and yell and point at the train wreck that awaited us if we didn't take action immediately, the train was moving at such a break-neck speed and with such force that its been virtually impossible to stop it or, for that matter, even slow it down so that we might build tracks up ahead. Only at the turn of the century and in the 2000 elections was the situation even made an issue. Unfortunately, it may have been too late.

Indeed, most independent analyst say that Social Security will be bankrupt by 2023. Some say even sooner. Of course, like those in 1941 who said that there was no way the Japanese would attack the United States, and those in the early 70s who said that the prospects of an debilitating energy crisis was simply foolishness, and more recently, those who say that global warming is the ridiculous rantings of tree-huggers and doomsday crackpots, there are those who suggest the predictions of doom for Social Security and Medicare and Medicaid are little more than the attempts of liberal politicians to increase the size of government. I would remind such skeptics of what Alan Greenspan himself, the head of the Federal Reserve and the man most responsible for our economic success, says about our current dilemma.

"There is no way to save Social Security without raising taxes or cutting benefits."

Boom. There it is. Plain and simple, and from the one man in the world who is most likely to know. As unbelievable as it sounds, both candidates running for president in the 2000 election arrogantly insisted that he's wrong. If Betty Crocker says her cake mix needs eggs or it won't work, who would argue?

There is talk—for the most part, irresponsible, half-baked proposals—of privatizing Social Security, of letting Generation Xers invest their own Social Security payments, of any number of things that will only serve to get a candidate a few votes and, if such proposals are adopted, expedite the bankruptcy of Social Security. It's rather like passing out umbrellas before a nuclear attack to keep the ashes from falling on our heads. It will not stop what is to come, but it will give us a false sense of security, perhaps even the satisfaction that at least we're addressing the problem, at least we're doing something.

That said, there are some proposals being floated around that do indeed have some potential. However this type of change would have to be gradual—perhaps even spread over three or four generations. Of course the government will have to shore up Social Security during this transition. To be sure, there's no easy fix.

Our Aging Society

In 1970, the median age began to rise as Baby Boomer parents began to age. Now, in the year 2001, the median

Dost thou love life? Then do not squander time; for that's the stuff life is made of.

—Benjamin Franklin

Anyone who isn't confused doesn't really understand the situation.

—Edward R. Murrow

age in our country is at thirty-six. By 2010 it will be 39, and by 2030, it will be forty-one. American elders outnumber American teenagers for the first time in history (approximately 15 percent of the population!).

Clearly our society is aging. The number of Americans over 65 has more than doubled since 1950. Today there are more than 35 million over 65—more than the population of Canada. By 2020, there will be 51 million Americans over the age of 65. The same youth culture that fueled the 60s social movements has aged and is now fueling an elderly culture that is obliterating the model for how the elderly are viewed. And why shouldn't it?

The U.S. is not just aging; the landscape of age is changing (behavioral changes). Old developmental psychology models are not so valid—or at least need to be interpreted/applied more loosely. Age is becoming a poor predictor of life events. People are starting families much later in life. Many parents and even grandparents are earning college and graduate degrees. Many aging people have begun to exercise, thus sustaining a more active and progressive lifestyle well into their seventies.

Big things are expected of us, and nothing big ever came of being small.

—Bill Clinton

Robert Maxwell, vice-president of the American Association of Retired Persons (AARP), says the script for each stage of human development keeps getting revised. "One result is that the stage directions and lines bequeathed to each generation by its predecessors often seem to be from another play, and each generation has to improvise. The process of aging has become different for each successive generation. The 70-year-old today is more like a person of 50 twenty years ago."

On Political and Economic Power

One of the most stunning results of the aging of our society is the political and economic empowerment of aging

Americans. Twenty-five percent of over-50 Americans own 75 percent of our assets and do half of our discretionary spending. Authors Jerry Gerber, Janet Wolff, Walter Klores and Gene Brown, in their book *Lifetrends: The Future of Baby Boomers and Other Aging Americans*, say that, "Baby Boomers will be a true revolutionary generation of elders. As elders, they will have unparalleled political and social clout."

SURE HE SAYS HE'S ON OUR SIDE NOW—IT'S AN ELECTION YEAR!

In the 90s, the median net worth of people in this age group was just over $60,000—double the average of all Americans. They constituted twelve percent of the population, but twenty-five percent of the federal budget went for their needs. Now, a little over a decade later, as the effects of our aging society are being felt and projections for the future are being made, the question that has followed us since 1946 must be answered: Will the children of the Baby Boomer generation feel obliged to contribute a substantial part of their income to entitlement programs for the increasing number of aging Baby Boomers in our society?

On the Next Generation Calling the Shots

The Baby Busters (a.k.a. the Reagan Generation or Generation X) were born after 1965. It was the first American generation smaller than the one that preceded it. It came of age in the 80s—the Reagan years, the ME Decade. Consequently, the values of that era have found their way into the philosophies of that generation. The result is that less importance has been placed on taking care of others—especially the old and infirm—via entitlement programs.

Harvard Economist Benjamin M. Friedman warns that, "by the time members of the [Baby Buster] generation are old enough to begin asking who was responsible for their diminished circumstances, they will not even know what they have lost."

Even more alarming, Friedman foresees Baby Boomers aging during a period of steady decline for the American economy.

On Problems the Aging Society Will Face

The first Baby Boomers will begin to retire in 2011. And they will keep retiring in even bigger droves for the next twenty years. Experts disagree on Boomers' future. Some forecasters predict Medicare collapses not too long after the turn of the century, and that Social Security will be gone around 2020. Baby Boomers are making socio-political choices today that will make their retirements difficult. Many are often disengaged politically—due in part to the pull-themselves-up-by-the-bootstraps philosophy.

Many conservative Baby Boomers are unwilling to finance Social Security, Medicare and Medicaid with their tax dollars for what they see as a socialist ideal that amounts to financing a welfare state. Their children, the Baby Busters, are even less engaged politically, and even less willing to have money taken out of their paychecks. The result is that it's very unlikely that a president, congressman or senator will get elected any time soon if he or she supports a tax increase to help pay for the entitlements due retiring Baby Boomers.

The single biggest problem that current and future retirees face is the drastically decreased number or workers entering the workforce and paying into entitlement programs designed to insure that retirees who helped build our society and its super-economy will be provided for in their golden years.

"You don't fix Social Security by putting money into it; you fix it by putting children into it so they can work and contribute to it in their parents' old age.... Boomers simply haven't had enough kids to do the job," says economist and financial analyst Jane Bryant Quinn.

Therein lies the dilemma we are face with as we begin the 21st century.

"It is not yet possible to determine who will be the last recipient of Social Security benefits," claims Peter Young of the Adam Smith Institute, "but it is fairly safe to say that he or she is alive today."

Social Security was established in 1935. Then there were 40 workers to pay taxes to support each retiree; now there are three workers per each retiree, and taxes have risen to meet costs. By 2011, ther could be as few as one worker per retiree. By the year 2020, under current policies, programs for older people will consume more than 65 percent of the federal budget.

Medicare was added in 1965, part of LBJ's Great Society program. Ironically, that very same year marked the beginning of a steadily declining birth rate. The Baby Boomer phenomenon was a demographic digression not likely to be repeated in our lifetime.

As a result, we are faced with a socio-economic problem for which there are no precedents, and which will (if we survive it) most likely never happen again—at least in our lifetimes. Because we as Americans have become complacent and, to a certain degree, disengaged from the management of our social economy, opting instead to leave the decision-making and planning up to ostensibly more informed and/or enlightened experts and leaders, we find ourselves at the mercy of whatever they say. Such complacency, historically speaking, has proven fatal to many a society.

The problems and issues that are confronting those of us who have begun to think about our retirements are worth noting—if for no other reason than to know what the informed and/or enlightened experts and leaders might—or at least should—be thinking about.

- workers born after 1960 will not be able to collect the full amount of benefits until 67
- qualifying age for full Social Security benefits will no doubt be raised because of the decreasing ratio of workers to retirees
- pensions will be less generous than current
- 401(k)s are subject/vulnerable to sharp decreases in the assets in which they are invested
- pensions cover only 43% of full-time employees in smaller businesses, compared with large organizations (80% of all employment is in firms with fewer than 100 people)
- during the stock market crash of Oct. 87, $210 billion worth of pension fund assets—almost ten percent of their portfolios—vanished
- despite federal guarantees of pensions under the Employee Retirement Income Security Act of 1974 (ERISA), widespread bankruptcies might make it difficult for the govt. to reimburse everybody completely
- pensions for workers who retire at 60 can end up costing a company twice as much as one for an employee who leaves at 65
- recent move by employers away from traditional defined benefit plans toward cash balance accounts, relieving employers of their responsibility to provide guaranteed lifetime income to their retired employees

All this will not be finished in the first 100 days. Nor will it be finished in the first 1,000 days, nor in the life of this Administration, nor even perhaps in our lifetime on this planet. But let us begin.

—John F. Kennedy

- o we will have to lessen penalties in lost Social Security benefits for those who work after retirement age

In the 60s, they led the revolution that changed society and the way it views its youth. In the latter decades of the 20th century, they changed the way we as a society viewed our role in world affairs. Why shouldn't this same generation change the way we view the elderly. As an allegory of evolving man, the Baby Boomer generation may be said to have lived a full, productive life. Indeed, it may forever be known as the generation that changed the world.

There's little argument that current and near-future retirees are responsible for the greatest period of human productivity in the history of the world. Unfortunately, our socio-political evolution has and appears that it will continue to steer away from public financing of their welfare during their golden years. There seems to me to be a fundamental question of fairness in this development—not to mention a subtle but unmistakable violation of the time-honored principle that one should honor one's mother and father. Nevertheless, the trend toward reducing what is now popularly called entitlements appears to be here to stay.

We have all been socialized in one way or another to believe that we reap what we sew. There is something about this idea that strikes a resonant chord deep within us. It is a subtle truth, a prescription for justice. It makes symmetrical sense. It is both a warning and a plan.

It is for precisely this reason that the idea of reaping what one has sewn is at the heart of my financial planning philosophy—The Master Plan. For it is becoming increasingly obvious that society will not be able to provide for us at the levels it has heretofore promised as we begin to leave the workforce and enjoy the best of our lives.

Consequently, we must prepare ourselves to reap what we have sewn.

In the following chapters I'll discuss important financial planning issues that will—regardless of the course our society and its political economy takes—enable us to do just that.

What is understood by republican government in the United States is the slow and quiet action of society upon itself.

—Alexis de Tocqueville

The Ballad of Bill and Betty Continues…

Bill had worked his way up to crew chief in a good company with a pension plan. By the time Bill, Jr. was a senior in high school and Nellie was a junior, they'd managed to save enough to pay for about half of their children's college—if they went to state schools. Of course they were both extremely bright and had a good chance to get scholarships.

Then, on a fresh spring day in 1984, the letter came: "State University is pleased to admit William Boomer, Jr. to its class of 1988." Unfortunately he wasn't offered any scholarships. He was, however, qualified for low interest guaranteed student loans. Bill and Betty were careful not let on that they were worried about paying for everything—about $25,000 per year. In fact, they even went so far as to tell Bill that all he had to do was worry about getting good grades. They would take care of the financial responsibilities.

And so they did—and could, for at least the next two years. After that, they didn't know what they would do. Bill kept his end of the bargain by finishing his first semester with a 3.7 GPA.

Then, in the spring of the next year, Nellie's letter came. She was admitted into Princeton's class of 1989.

Later they learned that she'd received several scholarships. Unfortunately the balance left to pay was still greater than the entire amount they'd have to pay for Bill Jr.'s state university education. They'd never realized how expensive an Ivy League education was. Of course they made her the same deal they made Bill Jr.—that they'd worry about paying for it—over $50,000 per year—if she concentrated on getting good grades.

The Boomers had always assumed that between pension and Social Security benefits, along with some money they'd put away and a few other small investments, their retirement would be OK. In fact, they often thought that they were ahead of the game since none of their friends seemed as prepared for retirement as they were. Of course none of their friends had Ivy League educations to pay for.

Needless to say, the Boomers were extremely proud of their children. They often mused that their children were proof that they themselves were smart and could have been rocket scientists if they'd wanted, but that they'd chosen a more demanding career: parenting. In fact, like many parents, they saw a good deal of themselves in their children. Bill, Jr. was a naturally happy young man, kind and patient, but would get terribly upset at injustice and unfairness in the world, and looked upon politicians and bureaucrats and the corporate community with disdain. He was like his mother.

Nellie, on the other hand, was a driven, determined young woman who sought out opportunity and excelled within the system. Though it was clear she would be much more successful in terms of wealth and position, she was like her father.

CHAPTER TWO

WHY AND WHEN FINANCIAL PLANNING IS IMPORTANT

A survey by the Center for Mature Consumer Studies indicated that 730 out of 1,000 respondents over the age of 55 were worried about maintaining financial independence. Still yet another study showed that six out of ten middle-class working Americans list "making sure I have a steady source of income when I retire" as their primary financial goal. The Social Security Administration published a report that says only four out of 100 Americans achieve financial independence by the age of sixty-five.

Most financial planners insist that the single biggest problem—and the number one cause for people not achieving their financial goals—is that they haven't done the proper planning for their financial future. Of course this shouldn't surprise anyone. Yet time and time again I come across individuals who are terribly distressed by their financial predicament, but can't for the life of them understand why they're in the situation they're in.

Planning for your financial independence is important for many reasons beyond the obvious one of having the financial wherewithal to do anything you want—all of which can improve the quality of your life.

Peace of Mind

The reward of a thing well done is to have done it.

—Ralph Waldo Emerson

First and foremost, successful financial planning can give you the peace of mind you need to enjoy life without the anxieties that almost always accompany an uncertain financial situation. How much of your life has been spent worrying about making ends meet and whether you're getting the best deal on your investment? Too often Americans (and people in general) miss out on important and significant events in their lives—and their family's lives—because they worry about their financial situation. Moreover, often one's financial anxieties can contribute to health problems—both mental and physical. I have encountered people who have allowed the stress from financial worries to exacerbate (and sometimes even cause) high blood pressure, ulcers, insomnia, heart problems and even mild cases of paranoia.

Psychologists agree that one of the keys to good mental health is being able to take control of the social environment in which you exist instead of letting the environment control you. By successfully planning your retirement, you do as much as can be done toward controlling the environment in which you exist.

He who desires but acts not breeds pestilence.

—William Blake

Sense of Security

Too often those of us who find ourselves approaching retirement age without having given financial planning much thought will begin to suffer a loss of security. Ironically, this is probably not so much a loss of security as it is a realization of one's own financial planning shortcomings. I liken it to a family who, assuming that hotel rooms will be plentiful, takes off on vacation without making reservations.

It is human nature to put things out of sight/out of mind. It frees up our psyches to address and deal with other things that are more immediate. It creates room in our personalities to live for today. Unfortunately this mentality is the number one reason that most people find themselves on the brink of retirement with little or no plan on how to at least sustain the sense of security that will enable them to enjoy their golden years. All too often in such cases, soon-to-be-retirees spend a good portion of their early retirement—what should be the most enjoyable time in their life—worrying about their financial situation and wondering about their future.

There is nothing quite like the sense of security that comes from knowing that your future is secure and your retirement can be everything you want it to be.

Self-Confidence

John P., a 59-year-old sales rep for a soap manufacturing company, realized that he was only five or six years away from retirement. Having always thought himself a master salesman, he never worried about retirement as he was certain that he would, by that time so far away in the future, have made his millions and could live comfortably in his golden years. However, the last few years hadn't been as fruitful as he thought they would (the emergence of the internet as a sales tool had taken a sizable chunk out of his business and limited his potential), and his children's college had cost more than he'd thought. Now he and his wife Carolyn had next to nothing stashed away, no plan whatsoever for retirement.

So distraught over the fact that he wasn't the breadwinner he thought he was, John P. all but quit. His self-confidence shattered and embarrassed, he couldn't bring himself to begin addressing the financial issues of retirement. Fortunately, Carolyn was able to persuade him that he'd done a wonderful job providing for his family; they'd lived comfortably, paid for both their children's college educations, and had been and still are the happiest family she knew. Perhaps even more importantly, however, she was able to persuade her husband that it wasn't too late to start planning for their retirement.

All too often, retirees—especially those who haven't done the proper financial planning—seem to lose the self-confidence they once had, and approach retirement with an almost defeatist attitude. Having a financial plan for retirement can give you the self-confidence to continue living the life that you want. Indeed, many retirees thrive when the problematic issues of financial security have been addressed. Some start successful businesses, some get involved in politics, some simply enjoy the fruits of their labor to the fullest.

Discipline

Another side-benefit that comes from having a sound financial plan in place for retirement is discipline. Any good plan for retirement will require a budget to be developed and require the discipline to stick to it. For some this is already second nature. For others, however, there's never been a better time to develop discipline than within the context of retirement planning.

Socio-Political Voice

A recent phenomenon that has businesses, politicians and policy-makers standing at attention is the newfound economic and political power that many retirement-aged Americans are wielding. By letting their money and investments speak for them and their social and political concerns, a traditionally under-represented and under-appreciated segment of society can voice their opinions and effect political and social change—not to mention their own financial success. Needless to say, corporate America is taking note.

Groups like the American Association of Retired Persons (AARP) are affecting substantial social and political change. An article in the *St. Petersburg Times* (Sunday, March 5, 2000) says that lawmakers are becoming frustrated at the AARP because they're cautious about whose Medicare drug plan they will throw their support behind, which would mean almost certain success for whomever's bill they choose. A spokesperson for the organization said they're weighing the options carefully because what might seem a good plan today, could be bad later. As a result of their numbers, affluence and collectively organized voice, the AARP is becoming one of the shrewdest and most powerful political groups in the U.S.

Take sides. Neutrality helps the oppressor, never the victim. Silence encourages the tormentor, never the tormented.

—Elie Wiesel

In addition to organizations like the AARP that wield collective bargaining power, there are also many businesses and companies that provide issue-oriented options in the products and services they provide. Some investment companies provide a "Green List" of companies who, for one reason or another, are socially responsible so that if a client is so compelled, he or she can invest in companies that demonstrate social or political ideals that they support.

I applaud this development in our economic system. By "putting our money where our mouth is," so to speak, our voice can be heard loud and clear—often times more loudly and clearly than a vote cast at the ballot box. Indeed, with the chaos that is sure to ensue as we decide what to do about the impending Social Security, Medicare and Medicaid disasters, it's imperative that we make our voices heard loud and clear, lest our interests be represented by those who do not necessarily have our best interests at heart.

Emotional Fulfillment

Finally, perhaps the most fundamental benefit that can be received is the emotional fulfillment that comes from participating in the success that you have helped build. It took long, hard work to build the American Dream that we now enjoy. That hard work should be rewarded. Often those who contributed to the growth of our society in such a profound way are emotionally disappointed and feel that they've been forgotten and are unappreciated. Successful retirement planning can restore the sense of belonging and reward the contributions of a lifetime that, in many cases, have been neglected and even ignored.

Liberty means responsibility. That is why most men dread it.

—George Bernard Shaw

When to Start Planning

Far too many of us do not think seriously about retirement planning until retirement is upon us. Americans have been conditioned to believe that anything is possible and that there will always be the time and opportunity to take care of those things later.

"We didn't realize that it was sneaking up on us so quickly."

While it's never too late to plan, waiting until retirement is upon you makes it more difficult since usually there are no wages or salaries supporting you while investments begin to pay off.

The time to start planning for your retirement is well before that day happens. I have clients that start preparing for retirement ten, fifteen, some even twenty years before the day comes. The important thing to remember is that the earlier you start, the more time your strategy will have to work for you. And the more time your strategy has to work for you, the more secure your retirement will be.

People Don't Know What They Really Don't Know

For of all the sad words of tongue or pen, the saddest are these: "It might have been!"

—John Greenleaf Whittier

There's an old saying that says the first thing you need to do before you can get smarter is realize how much you don't know. No where is this more true than in planning your retirement. With politicians scrambling for votes by passing fashionable and high-profile quick-fix measures to take advantage of media attention on a given issue, new tax laws that change the dynamics of tried and true investments, not to mention scheme-like opportunities from all manner of financial gurus, the importance of understanding the financial planning landscape, and being aware of all the options and variables cannot be overstated.

Take Leonard W. He and his wife Marion owned a couple of rental properties and a few stable blue chip stocks. The income that they received from these investments was steady but not very substantial. They calculated that their homemade retirement plan was earning enough to just about sustain them in two years when Leonard would retire from his job with United Postal Service.

They thought about consulting a retirement planner to help them organize a strategy that will do more than just sustain them. But then came the dot-com phenomenon. Millionaires—even billionaires—were made seemingly overnight. He'd seen the effect TV had on the economy and consumer culture in general. Marketing was revolutionized; salesmen became little more than order-takers. Sure it was the death of Willie Loman. But it was the birth of a great economic boom. It took very little time for Leonard to realize that this was where his money should be.

To make a long story short, while he picked a relatively stable stock, he got in late. The software company he invested in was purchased by a larger company who, after a buying spree of smaller start-ups to insure their cutting edge technology and position in the quickly plateauing market, lost 65 percent of its value when it was discovered that they had illegally acquired several smaller companies and were, in effect, trying to create a monopoly in that particular niche of the software industry. The government handed down the largest fine in history at that point, and ordered the company to sell off the companies in question.

Remember that time is money.

—Benjamin Franklin

Needless to say, Leonard lost the shirt he would have worn in retirement. The tragedy was that it could have been avoided had he known more about the dynamics of this hyper-growth industry and the stage of the business cycle it was in.

Consider this analogy: Not long ago, some government employees decided to conduct a controlled burn in the dry mountains of northern New Mexico. After setting the fire to burn off scrub and other fire hazards, the wind changed directions and the fire quickly got out of control. By the time it was under control again, thousands of acres were destroyed, and hundreds of homes in Los Alamos were burned to the ground. Mightn't such a tragedy have been avoided had those involved taken a little more time to study the weather and conditions?

The dot-com/software/internet phenomenon was indeed an economic marvel. Unfortunately, those who jumped on the bandwagon too late or who didn't take the time to learn about the products and services that were being developed, were introduced to the dark side of the marvel. Many of these were seniors who had seen the phenomenon before, and who were set on getting their piece of the golden pie.

We are indeed fully enveloped in the information age. One has only to look so far as the dot-com industry to see that information is, in fact, currency in this age. If you don't have millions in cash when you retire, at least have millions in information. Thus prepared, you're ready to put a plan into action.

People Don't Plan To Fail; They Fail To Plan

When, in the late fall of 1941, commanders at Pearl Harbor were informed that the base was a prime and likely target for Japanese attacks, they paid little attention to the warnings and made no plans for such a scenario. We all know what happened next.

Nobody would accuse the commanders at Pearl Harbor or the American forces of planning for failure. They did, however, fail to plan. The same can be said about people in general. Nobody plans to fail; they simply fail to plan which, often times, leads to failure.

This, more than any other single thing, is the biggest tragedy in retirement strategies. Too often, people see financial planners as quacks and charlatans whose only concern is to get their hands on old peoples' money. While there are certainly quacks and charlatans out there who operate like that, the good ones—the real ones—will help their clients plan their retirement by analyzing their particular situations and examining all the options and variables available to them, and plan against unforeseen social and economic forces that could effect the success of their retirement strategy.

Certainly no reasonable person would dispute the fact that the better the plan, the better the result. Unfortunately, and even tragically in some cases, we've become so caught up in the hyper-active socio-economic climate of our times, that we neglect the fundamentals. In this computer age, we're encouraged to plug the variables into a fool-proof software program developed by a former religious guru and then sit back and watch yourself get rich. And then there are the celebrity/sports star testimonials: "It worked for me; it'll work for you, too!"

Real life, hands-on, thoughtful planning has become a lost art. Planning is at the heart of what I do. Planning is where I make a difference. Real life, hands-on, thoughtful planning is what you can't get from a software program. Given a certain level of competence in the use of basic financial instruments and a knowledge of how they might perform, the actual financial results a person is likely to see will be very similar to what a computer software program or any one of hundreds or even thousands of other financial planners might generate. The difference is made in the planning.

Planning takes good listening skills, good communication skills, and above all, thoughtful contemplation of one's particular situation. Thoughtful planning can mean thousands of dollars. A good financial planner will help a client anticipate unforeseen expenses from life experiences that don't readily plug into a software program. Proactive hedges against inflation, thoughtful investments that may

A wrong decision isn't forever; it can be reversed. The losses from a delayed decision are forever; the can never be retreived.

—John Kenneth Galbraith

be better insulated against the downside of current and future trends, insurance and healthcare options that minimize financial and emotional costs—no matter what the scenario. The art of planning is not just identifying what you want to do and how you want to do it. It's planning for what you *might* have to do and how you *might* have to do it. Planning for any case or scenario is not excessive planning. Indeed, it's fundamental, basic planning—and absolutely necessary if one is to get the most out of retirement. It can mean the difference between just being retired and living the kind of retirement you've always dreamed about.

The Ballad of Bill and Betty Boomer Continues…

With the kids both in school now, Bill and Betty were able to sit down and think about their finances. They didn't tell Bill, Jr. or Nellie that they had decided to take out a second mortgage on the house to cover their college expenses. They also didn't tell their kids that the construction company Bill, Sr. worked for had been sold and his new employer is converting its pensions to cash balance accounts, nor that his employment status was uncertain. They also didn't tell their children about Betty's diagnosis—a minor illness—but one that would require expensive medication for the rest of her life.

Now Bill is hearing that he won't be eligible for all the Medicare, Medicaid and Social Security benefits he thought he would be eligible for. Betty blames it all on the Republicans; Bill sees a conspiracy of much larger proportions. He has begun to see the results of the unfettered and unchecked economic policies of the American Dream.

"Let the old people fend for themselves!" he would grumble if ever the subject were brought up on card night.

Then early one sunny Saturday morning, they got a phone call from Nellie. She's getting married.

At the end of your life you will never regret not having passed one more test, winning one more verdict or not closing one more deal. You will regret time not spent with a husband, a child, a friend or a parent.

—Barbara Bush

CHAPTER THREE

THE MASTER PLAN

Knowledge itself is power.

—Francis Bacon

The dictionary defines "master plan" as a plan giving overall guidance. I would give this definition a little more specificity and focus: an indisputable universal axiom that reveals truth and gives overall guidance.

The idea that one reaps what one has sewn is just such an axiom. It expresses a universal truth, and suggests between its lines a plan for success—assuming, of course, that one sees success as something noble and worthy of pursuing. This indisputable universal axiom is at the heart of my financial planning philosophy, and the foundation upon which the plan that I use to help those of us approaching retirement age to achieve financial independence is built. Based upon the idea that you reap what you sew, The Master Plan provides both a context and method for realizing both your human and financial potential.

But before you begin to reap what you have sewn, you need to gather as much information as possible on various financial options and variables. Familiarize yourself with what's out there. Understand your choices. No plan in the world will work as well as it should without at least a fundamental understanding of the elements that are involved in it. For some this may mean seeking professional financial planning advice. For others, it may mean doing some investigation and research. In the pages that follow, I'll briefly discuss many of the most important options and variables that come into play when planning your financial future.

If one does not know to which port one is sailing, no wind is favorable.

—Seneca ("the Younger")

That said, in order to reap what you have sewn, the first element of the Master Plan is to establish where you are today—both financially and personally. Assess your net worth.

Assessing Your Personal and Financial Net Worth

You're at a dinner given by your soon-to-be-former employer. You're sitting at the head table along with your spouse, your boss and his spouse, and several friends who are waiting their turn to speak. One after another, your friends and colleagues step up to the podium and, without a second thought, mercilessly blurt stories about you—some true, some not—into the microphone.

By the time your closest friend finishes telling the story about the time you smashed into the car in front of you because you thought the light had changed since the cars next to you in the left hand turn lane had started to move, and suggested that it was a perfect example of how scatter-brained and clueless you are when it comes to the real world, you're starting to wonder about the little half-truths that most jokes and jibes contain. On your way home that night, the little truths gain power and you start to wonder about what you've accomplished, whether you're really as scatter-brained and oblivious to the passing of time as your best friend said, and whether you really were as important an employee as your boss said you were in his closing remarks. The pension he's giving you doesn't seem as thankful as his remarks. In fact, it won't even cover your expenses—at least for the next ten years until your house is paid off. To top it all off, the gold watch without any numbers on the face that they gave you for your years of loyal, dedicated service is only gold-plated.

Often times the aging process itself can have a negative effect on one's emotional health. Add to that a social environment that is increasingly insensitive to its own progenitors and the sacrifices they made in order to build the great socio-economic monolith that we now live in, and the low self-esteem and feelings of inconsequence and insignificance that social scientists say many aging people undergo is more the norm than the exception. Such an emotional state can cause many older folks to address retirement planning with less than adequate enthusiasm and result in financial mistakes.

The first and foremost piece of advice that I would offer up is don't believe the hype. Throughout history the young have discounted the older members of their society and ascribed to them a diminishment of capacities that marks them as over-the-hill, washed up, missing some tools in the shed. America has all but perfected this phenomenon. Indeed, one of our most important (if not misunderstood) contributions to the development of culture is the creation of a robust, almost unchecked youth culture. In fact, the youth culture that we planted and nourished—albeit more out of economic motivation than any sort of responsible social vision—has evolved to the point of having an almost tyrannical hold on what is normal and desirable in our society.

According to *The Social Psychology of Aging*, negative stereotypes of the aging population, while common in the past, are changing. Past stereotypes of the elderly as unhappy, in poor health, and lonely do not match the reality of life for the majority of the aging population.

Indeed, despite unconscionable political dilly-dallying with legislation that, ostensibly, would benefit our aging society, there is overwhelming evidence that our aging population is more sophisticated in almost every area of our social existence than it has ever been. And why wouldn't it be? That historically large and successful segment of our population has witnessed first-hand the social processes of the American Dream during its most illustrious period. They've seen the vast fortunes acquired, the sprawling growth, the widening gap between the wealthy and the poor, the social disintegration of the values passed on from a simpler, less-frenetic time. Gone is the caution and lessons learned from the Great Depression. The vast majority of the movers and shakers of our current socio-economic environment have never seen widespread poverty and unemployment. The closest thing to hard times that they have known was the 70s gasoline shortage when the price of gas shot up, in relative terms, to about what it shot up to at the turn of the century.

As for the mindset that seems to be firmly entrenched into the collective consciousness of our youthful society, there's little to suggest that it understands the dynamics of the ship it has been entrusted with sailing, or the scope of the impact that decisions the captain and crew have made in the last 30 years have had and will continue to have. Indeed, perhaps our greatest hope lies in the experiential knowledge and the time-tempered view that our aging population has of the world they built and of the generations to which they've given birth. If we're to continue on our unprecedented path of success as a society, we must incorporate the knowledge and wisdom of those who not only designed our world, but experienced it. Indeed, our willingness to invite the contributions that our aging population have to offer is a fair measure of our willingness to approach our full potential as a great society.

So before you ride off willy-nilly into the sunset and sign up for this investment and that insurance policy and any one of a number of financial opportunities designed specifically with the retiree in mind, take stock in yourself. Chances are that you have seen more of and understand better the world we live in than those who insist upon describing and explaining it to you. Your experience matters; your knowledge matters; your wisdom matters. And don't let the psychic fodder of the hyperactive, economics-driven society that we have become suggest differently.

A man's character is his fate.

—Heraclitus

I TOLD HIM THAT CAR WAS A LEMON, BUT HE BOUGHT IT ANYWAY. WHAT DO I KNOW—I'M AN OLD MAN. NO ONE LISTENS TO ME ANYMORE.

As for assessing your financial situation, the following Net Worth Worksheet will help you calculate where you stand.

ASSETS

1. Cash in Hand

current checking account balance	________
current savings account balance	________
money market funds	________
cash surrender value of insurance policies	________
other assets	________

2. Income-producing Investments

certificates of deposit	________
money market instruments	________
treasury bills, notes and bonds	________
municipal bonds	________
corporate bonds	________
notes receivable	________
mutual funds	________
investment trusts	________
trust deeds/mortgages receivable	________
other assets	________

3. Growth Investments

real estate	
residence	________
rental property	________
stocks	________
stock mutual funds	________
business ownership	________
partnership investments	________
collectibles	
gold	________
silver	________
gemstones	________
rare coins	________
rare stamps	________

antiques ________
fine art ________
other assets ________

4. Retirement Assets
individual retirement accounts ________
pension benefits ________
Keough plan/Simple IRA ________
annuities ________
employee savings plan ________
deferred compensation plan (401(k)) ________
employee stock-option plan (ESOP) ________
other assets ________

5. Personal Assets
furnishings ________
cars ________
jewelry ________
musical instruments ________
stereos, TVs, VCRs, cameras ________
tools and equipment ________
clothing ________
other assets ________

TOTAL ASSETS $____________

LIABILITIES

1. Short-term liabilities (due within one year)
unpaid bills ________
outstanding credit card balances ________
unpaid taxes ________
other short-term obligations ________

2. Long-term liabilities (due in one year or more)

mortgage loans outstanding	________
home equity loans outstanding	________
automobile loans outstanding	________
charge accounts/installment loans outstanding	________
margin due on stocks	________
life insurance loans	________
other long-term obligations	________

TOTAL LIABILITIES $____________

NET WORTH $____________
(total assets minus total liabilities)

Setting Goals

Man is still the most extraordinary computer of all.

—John F. Kennedy

Now that you know where you stand personally and financially, it's time to set some realistic goals for yourself—both personally and financially—that will facilitate personal growth. How have you dealt with the chaos that outside forces wreak on your personality? Where do you want to be emotionally and/or spiritually during the best years of your life? Are you being challenged mentally and intellectually? What about your physical health? Are you satisfied with your physical condition?

Most people have spent the better part of their wage-earning years worrying about bills and expenses, the health and welfare of kids and aging parents. Few of us want to continue the frenetic, worrisome lifestyle that is part and parcel of that stage of our lives. Furthermore, few of us have had the occasion to give much thought to our personal health and well-being during retirement.

As with anything else, old habits are difficult to change. If we don't give these important aspects of our life any thought, chances are we will continue to live at the mercy of outside forces—no doubt for most of us, one of the most frustrating things about our wage-earning years. Before you make plans that will affect your financial well-being during retirement, take the time to discover what it is that makes you happy and content, challenged and fulfilled.

Now that you've thought about and set some personal goals for yourself, establish your financial goals. First of all, think of common life events that cost money and affect you financially.

o career change
o retirement
o return to work
o unemployment
o relocation
o divorce
o widowhood
o remarriage
o disability or illness
o caring for a dependent spouse or parent

Now determine which events might apply to you and set financial goals that will help you weather the transitions smoothly. Use the following Financial Goals Worksheet to record your financial goals and the costs associated with them.

Experience is the name everyone gives to their mistakes.

—Oscar Wilde

Date________

	Goals	Est. Cost	Financial Plan	Target Date
Short-	____	______	_________	________
term	____	______	_________	________
	____	______	_________	________
	____	______	_________	________
Inter-	____	______	_________	________
mediate	____	______	_________	________
	____	______	_________	________
	____	______	_________	________
Long-	____	______	_________	________
term	____	______	_________	________
	____	______	_________	________
	____	______	_________	________

Develop a Budget

You've assessed your net worth and set goals. Now it's time to develop a budget that will help you achieve your goals. A budget can help you avoid money problems and steer you toward your financial goals by:

- o telling you whether you're living within your means
- o forcing you to make conscious decisions about expenditures
- o pinpointing any expenses you need to trim
- o helping you establish priorities
- o allowing you to set aside a sum each month for savings

Budgeting is particularly important for retirees and soon-to-be-retirees for two reasons:

1) income may drop overnight following two common place events: widowhood and retirement

2) many retirees are house-rich but cash-poor

Living within your budget requires discipline and confidence. These tips will help you trim expenses and live comfortably within your budget.

- Plan a regular savings program.

- Set aside 5 – 15% of gross income for savings and investing (between the ages of 50 and retirement, set aside 15 – 20%). With steady saving, even modest sums result in big payoffs over time. Albert Einstein was once asked what the most powerful force in the world was. He replied, "Compound interest."

- Create an emergency fund to cover unanticipated expenses such as those that would follow a major illness or loss of job. For older adults, the fund should total six months' living expenses and should be readily available.

- Anticipate larger expenses in advance and set aside money each month to cover them. Open a special account (an impound account) to cover fixed expenses that you pay quarterly, semiannually, or annually. These might include homeowners and auto insurance premiums, property tax, and federal and state income tax. Total the annual cost of these items and divide by 12. The result is the amount you should deposit each month.

- Avoid fads and impulse buying.

- Limit purchases of expensive items by substituting similar but less costly ones where possible—keeping in mind, of course, that there is no substitute for quality and value.

- o Take advantage of clearance and holiday sales.
- o Use senior citizen discounts whenever possible.
- o Comparison shopping.
- o Avoid buying on credit.

Often my clients don't even know where the money they spend goes. I have discovered a "down and dirty" method that almost always awakens them to holes in their planning. First, add up combined monthly net income. After determining that sum, I'll ask them how much they have left over in their checking accounts after they pay their bills, taxes and set aside something for their retirement savings. Often the answer is "zero." People almost always underestimate what they spend.

The following budget worksheet will help you examine your particular situation.

EXPENSES

	Anticipated Expenses	**Actual Expenditures**
Shelter		
rent or mortgage pmt.	______	______
property taxes	______	______
property insurance	______	______
maintenance	______	______
gas, oil, electricity	______	______
telephone	______	______
water and sewer	______	______

Food

groceries	________	________
eating out	________	________
other	________	________

Transportation

car payments	________	________
gasoline, oil, etc.	________	________
maintenance, repair	________	________
insurance	________	________
public transportation	________	________
taxes and fees	________	________
vehicle registration	________	________

Clothing

new purchases	________	________
dry cleaning/laundry	________	________
other	________	________

Health Care

insurance	________	________
physicians/dentists	________	________
hospital costs	________	________
drugs	________	________
glasses, contacts	________	________
other	________	________

Personal Care

hair care	________	________
toiletries	________	________
other	________	________

Recreation

vacations	________	________
recreational equipment	________	________
recreational activities	________	________

movies, theatres	________	________
newspapers, books, etc.	________	________
club dues	________	________
other	________	________
Gifts and Contributions		
religious and charities	________	________
political causes	________	________
family gifts	________	________
holiday gifts	________	________
other	________	________
Savings		
savings accounts	________	________
life insurance	________	________
disability insurance	________	________
investments	________	________
employee savings plans	________	________
profit-sharing plans	________	________
pensions	________	________
annuities	________	________
IRAs	________	________
retirement contrib.	________	________
other	________	________
Obligations		
pet expenses	________	________
credit card pmts.	________	________
federal income tax	________	________
state income tax	________	________
other debt pmts.	________	________
Total Monthly Expenses	________	________

INCOME

	Anticipated Income	Actual Income
all salaries and wages	________	________
dividends/interest	________	________
pension	________	________
social security	________	________
gifts	________	________
other	________	________
Total Monthly Income	________	________

The Ballad of Bill and Betty Boomer Continues…

Feeling exhausted and as if they've been spinning their wheels all their lives, Bill and Betty had begun to think that they were never going to get to a place where they could enjoy life. They felt that for every step forward, they took two steps back. It seemed as though they'd spent their whole lives reacting to external events instead of listening to their inner voices and following their bliss. Not that they didn't cherish the life they had, but there seemed to be so much more that they wanted to do. It seemed to them that their dreams were on hold, that their lives were on hold.

Feeling somewhat less than the superheroes they secretly thought they were, they decided to sit down and figure out what they'd done with their lives. What they needed was to take a deep breath and look at their situation through a filter of common sense.

They were 54 years old, owned their own home in a nice, quiet neighborhood; had put both kids in orthodontic braces when they needed them, had been to hundreds, perhaps even thousands of little league games and piano recitals and school plays; and had put both children through college—though they were still paying off the student loans that had allowed them to do that. And until recently, they had always been in excellent health.

Betty had been diagnosed with a minor albeit chronic lung ailment that required expensive medicine, and Bill's back had started to hurt him almost all the time, although he had put off and put off seeing a doctor.

And until recently, they had always felt secure as far as Bill's employment. The company at which he had worked for over thirty years had been purchased by a larger company and was in deep trouble with the government over the way they did business. It was almost as if the world had begun to conspire against them. Bill had always wanted to retire at 60 so he and Betty would still have time to enjoy life while they were still young enough. They had always wanted to take a month-long European vacation. They had always wanted to build a log cabin in the mountains and do nothing all day long but watch the sun come up and then set. Now they would be lucky if they could afford to pay this month's cable TV bill.

Of course they quickly steered away from this kind of defeatist attitude—something they had gone to great pains to teach their children. It was really very easy for them to focus on their success. There was a portrait of each of their children hanging over the fireplace in the living room, so they were never very far from their thoughts. Indeed, their children were the most important things in their life. By Bill and Betty's way of thinking, they had accomplished exactly what they had always wanted. They had two wonderful children who called home every week—and not collect. Nobody had better children than theirs.

They were not only determined to pay for Nellie's wedding, but to do it up right.

Some simple arithmetic, however, opened up their eyes to the immediacy and urgency of their financial situation—and not just for Nellie's wedding.

CHAPTER FOUR

ASSESSING SOURCES OF INCOME

So now you're thinking seriously about planning for your retirement. Good. What you need to do now is to examine your sources of income so you can effectively plan in advance and gather information in order to avoid painful surprises.

Over the past few years, there have been more laws, acts and legislation passed dealing with this, that and the other aspect of Social Security than any normal human could keep up with—which is precisely the plan. Numb the public with complicated, mind-boggling fluff, and they'll soon give in to exhaustion and go along with whatever happens. This "tinkering" with our Social Security system—for the most part, expedient political posturing by unscrupulous politicians who care more about reelection than what they're doing to the economic environment, and older Americans, in particular—has already threatened the solvency of one of our most successful American institutions. Add to that the imminent retire-

It could probably be shown by facts and figures that there is no distinctly native American criminal class except Congress.

—Mark Twain

For forms of government let fools contest; What'er is best administered is best.

—Alexander Pope

ment of the Baby Boomers and both the loss of their payments into the system and their collection of payments due them, and any number of other short-sighted economic policy decisions intended to bolster confidence in our economy that our government has made and is making, and what we're faced with is a recipe for an economic disaster that threatens our very socio-cultural existence.

The Social Security legislation of 1983 increased taxes on earned income, taxed Social Security benefits, and raised the eligibility age for full benefits after the year 2000. This incredibly dangerous policy of perpetually delaying the inevitable while chipping away at what older Americans are entitled to is inexcusable and may very well jeopardize the economic security of a whole generation, and perhaps a whole society and culture. Every session, it seems, some cosmetic remedy to squelch the doomsayers' TV time and thus public interest in the subject is debated until political posturing and Capitol Hill business-as-usual kills any substantial action. The public hears a lot about it, sees politicians waving their arms and beating their chests about it, and assumes that it has been addressed. But it hasn't.

Meanwhile, the amount of benefits you'll receive is slowly being decreased while the number of retirees is about to drastically increase. It's as if the politicians who are running the show—who are reaping the vast, unprecedented economic rewards that their parents have sewn—have decided that all the Baby Boomers are wealthy and therefore do not need what is rightfully theirs!

What then shall we do?

Hedge your bets.

In this chapter, I'll examine the most common sources of income for most people in their later years: Social Security, supplemental security income (SSI), and employee pensions (including "do-it-yourself" pensions).

Social Security

Are Social Security benefits the only source of income I'll need when I retire?

You'd be surprised to know that many people, for what ever reason, have it in their heads that Social Security benefits are the only source of income they'll need when they retire. These benefits are not now, nor were they when the program was established in 1935, intended to replace their earnings. And if current trends and patterns hold, the dollar value of benefits relative to the cost of living in our increasingly expensive culture will decrease. That's why it's so important to plan to supplement Social Security benefits with savings, pensions, investments and other income.

We must indeed all hang together, or, most assuredly, we shall all hang separately.

—Benjamin Franklin

How do I estimate my monthly benefit amount?

It's very simple to estimate the monthly benefit amount you'll be entitled to. If you're over 60, call your local Social Security office and ask for it. If you're under 60, ask the office for a Request for Earnings and Benefit Estimate Statement. Since the more information you have when planning your retirement, the more likely you are to be successful, this statement can be invaluable.

When and how do I apply for benefits?

Many older people have never really given a lot of thought to their retirement, and even less, for whatever reasons, to the idiosyncrasies of Social Security. For many, it's simply a matter of putting it off and putting it off until, all too soon, retirement is upon them. Others, though, never imagined that they would have to rely on Social Security as a source of income. Invariably, they find themselves in the uncomfortable position of having little or no idea of when and how to apply for benefits.

Quite simply, you should apply for Social Security benefits at least three months before your retire. It falls upon the retiree to initiate the process. Predictably, the government will not track you down to give you what is rightfully yours.

You'll need the following documents to apply:

- Social Security card
- birth certificate or other proof of age
- evidence of recent earnings (i.e., your last W-2, or a copy of your self-employment tax return)
- proof of your spouse's or ex-spouse's death if you are applying for survivors' benefits

Many older Americans never imagined that they would have to rely on Social Security as a source of income.

I GUESS WE ALWAYS THOUGHT WE'D BE RICH BY THE TIME WE WERE READY TO RETIRE....

At what age can I receive retirement benefits?

Most people qualify for full benefits at the age of sixty-five. However there are early and late retirement options that can affect the amount of benefits you receive. Those who retire at 62 will have their benefits reduced by about 20% because they will be receiving an additional 36 payments. Those who retire later will receive higher benefit payments—up to eight percent more each year until the year 2008. Beginning in 2000, the age at which full benefits are payable will gradually increase from 65 until it reaches 67 in 2022. Reduced benefits will still be available at age 62, but the reduction will also be larger.

Will a return to work affect the amount I receive in benefits?

If you return to work after you start receiving benefits, you will lose $1 for every $3 you earn above the annual exempt amount. Beginning in 2000, the age at which the earnings test applies will gradually increase as the retirement age rises.

Are my benefits taxable?

Unfortunately, in many cases they are—a thinly disguised attempt by the government to make it seem like they're giving you more than they are. In fact, up to one-half of your benefits may be subject to federal income tax if half your benefits plus all your non-Social Security income exceed a base amount. The base amount changes each year, so check with your local Social Security office for the current amount and specific stipulations.

What about survivor benefits?

If you are widowed you may qualify for Social Security survivor benefits based on the earnings record of your deceased spouse. Even if you are divorced you may qualify for benefits, provided the marriage lasted at least ten years. Call your local Social Security office for details.

"Understand what you own."

—Peter Lynch

Supplemental Security Income (SSI)

According to a survey sponsored by the American Association of Retired Persons (AARP), almost half of the older persons eligible for Supplementary Security Income

(SSI) do not receive benefits because they are unaware of the program or do not know how to apply. SSI is an income-support program run by the Social Security Administration that provides monthly cash payments to low-income adults over 65 or to people of any age who are blind or disabled. This income support is above and beyond what you may already be receiving. Check with your Social Security office for eligibility requirements (they vary from state to state).

Pensions

Many people who have been at the same job for an extended period of time may not know very much about the specifics of their pension plan. To find out important information that will help in your retirement planning, such as what type of plan you're covered by, what benefits you're entitled to, how much you'll receive at retirement, whether you'll receive payments or a lump sum, or whether your spouse is protected, consult your plan administrator and ask for a summary plan description, a summary annual report, and information about survivor coverage.

Most pension plans fall into one of the two following categories:

1) defined benefit
2) defined contribution

Most employees are covered by the first plan. They receive a specified monthly benefit at retirement. Many plans will pay a certain amount for each year of service. Some, however, pay a fixed dollar amount.

Defined contribution plans, however, do not promise to pay a predetermined benefit. Instead, the employer contributes a fixed amount to the employees account (perhaps five percent of annual earnings). At retirement, the employee receives the total contribution, plus any investment returns, usually in a lump sum or annuity.

Participation in a pension plan doesn't always mean an employee will receive benefits from it.

Individual Retirement Plans

Many employees have programs to help workers save for retirement. Often these "do-it-yourself" plans are offered in addition to regular pensions. In smaller companies, however, they may be the primary retirement program. In addition, you can create your own pension through contributions to a special account whether your employer offers retirement benefits or not.

Individual Retirement Accounts

Workers can contribute up to $2,000 a year and defer paying taxes on earnings from this money until they withdraw it. In some cases, all or part of the contribution is tax deductible. IRAs may be set up instead of or in addition to any pension plan your employee offers.

The rules for IRA distribution are strict. There is a 10 percent penalty for early withdrawal before age 59 and a half (in addition to any tax owed on the income). Also, you must start distributions before age 70 and a half (to avoid penalties, these withdrawals cannot fall below a certain amount—the minimum amount is calculated each year by dividing your life expectancy, as reported in IRS mortality tables, into the total amount in your IRA). The idea is that all of your IRA contributions will be distributed during your lifetime. If you want to stretch withdrawals over a longer period, you can calculate minimum distributions using the joint life expectancy of yourself and your IRA's designated beneficiary.

You can invest IRA funds in almost anything: stocks, bonds, mutual funds, money market funds, and certificates of deposit are some of the more common options. To find out if your IRA contribution is tax deductible, contact the IRS or your tax advisor.

I DON'T MIND TELLING YOU, IT WAS A REAL EYE-OPENER—THAT THE GOVERNMENT HAS A DATE THEY EXPECT ME TO LIVE TO...

The following "20 Crucial IRA Tips," from the February 2000 issue of *Mutual Funds* magazine, can help you get the most out of your IRAs.

1. Individual Retirement Accounts.
Once you've maxed out your employer's qualified retirement plan, it's time to consider an IRA. Traditional IRAs come in two flavors: deductible and non-deductible. Both offer tax-deferred growth. Roth IRAs, named for William J. Roth, their chief cheerleader in the Senate, also come in two versions: regular and conversion. Both offer tax-free growth.

2. Traditional IRAs.
Want an immediate tax deduction? Open an old-fashioned IRA. Be aware, though, that if you are covered by a retirement plan at work, an adjusted gross income (AGI) of $41,000 ($61,000 for a couple) will make you ineligible to make deductible contributions to an IRA. Not covered by a retirement plan where you work? Then it makes no difference how sizable your income is. You are eligible to make a deductible contribution.

However, to contribute to a traditional IRA, you do have to earn something. "Earned income," in this instance, includes taxable alimony but not nontaxable child support or unemployment compensation. And, of course, you must be younger than 70 and a half.

3. Spousal IRAs.
Many couples who are ineligible for deductible IRAs can qualify for a spousal IRA. The AGI limit is considerably higher for a deductible contribution to a spousal IRA by someone who is not employed but whose spouse is covered by some kind of retirement plan. Deductibility starts to phase out when AGI tops $150,000, and vanishes when it tops $160,000.

Under these rules, a stay-at-home spouse without a job can make a deductible contribution of as much as $2,000. This holds true whether the at-home spouse is unemployed (and looking for work), never employed, or retired, assuming he or she is under age 70 and a half.

4. Deadline.
You have until the day that IRS Form 1040 is due, April 15, to open an IRA and deposit your money. Even if you get an extension on the date your tax return is due, the April 15 IRA deadline holds.

5. Early withdrawals from an IRA.
Not until you begin withdrawals is there a reckoning with the IRS. Withdrawals of earning or deductible contributions are taxed as ordinary income. (Note that this applies even if your money was invested in tax-free municipal bonds, which is why you should never put such investments in an IRA.)

Withdrawals made before you reach age 59 and a half, though, are subject not only to the taxes that would ordinarily be due, but also to a penalty—ten percent of the amount you're taking out. The penalty will not be charged if you die or are permanently disabled, or if you're withdrawing the money to pay for college, qualified medical expenses, health-insurance premiums while you're unemployed, or to buy your first home.

6. Late IRA withdrawals.
The IRS also imposes a penalty for late withdrawals from your IRA. This one kicks in if you fail to start taking out the minimum required amount of money by April 1 of the year following the year you turn 70 and a half. Minimum distributions for subsequent years must be made by Dec. 31.

You can always remove funds faster than required, but failure to take at least the minimum means the IRS will hit you up for 50 percent of the difference between what you actually took and what you should have taken (a set amount based on your life expectancy or, if you so elect, the combined life expectancies of you and your spouse).

7. Don't delay that first distribution.
It can prove costly to delay the first required distribution until April of the following year, even though you're allowed to. Suppose you turn 70 and a half in 2000, and put off the first withdrawal until 2001. You will have to make a second withdrawal sometime in 2001, and the two combined could not only boost your income into a higher tax bracket, but also subject more of your Social Security payments to income tax.

8. Another reason not to delay.
In addition, making two withdrawals that first year might cause you to forfeit a valuable tax benefit. Many states allow a sizable annual exclusion—meaning escape from taxes—for distributions from IRAs and other retirement plans. For instance, New York's exclusion is $20,000 for each spouse. Delay your first withdrawal, and you lose that first year's exclusion.

9. Roth IRAs: The bad news.
Contributions to a Roth IRA do not reduce your income for tax purposes, as they are made with after-tax dollars. But they do provide some serious advantages.

10. Roth IRAs: The good news.
For starters, you can withdraw money you contributed to your Roth account at any time for any reason without tax or penalty.

Earnings, too, are tax-free, no matter how much an account has swelled, as long as you wait at least five years after opening the account and, generally, as long as you are at least 59 and a half. Unlike traditional IRAs, Roth withdrawals will not trigger taxes on otherwise tax-free Social Security benefits.

11. Eligibility.

Another difference: Roth IRAs permit you to keep making contributions as long as you or your spouse has income from any kind of job (not including income from investments). However, you become ineligible to make Roth contributions if your AGI tops $110,000 ($160,000 when filing a joint return).

12. Roth conversions: See the light.

With an AGI of less than $100,000, you have the option of converting your traditional IRA into a Roth, and thus avoiding taxes on any future withdrawals. The money you convert is not counted toward this $100,000 cap.

13. Roth conversions: Taxes.

Such conversions come with a price tag: Assuming that all of the money in your original IRA came from deductible contributions, you will pay taxes on the entire amount you are converting to a Roth, and you'll pay at your ordinary-income rate, regardless of when you opened the original IRA account. Ouch.

14. Roth conversions: The route to redemption.

This tax is due in the year you make the conversion, and a really painful situation could arise if, by the time you come to pay your taxes, stock prices and mutual fund NAVs are considerably lower than they were when you made the conversion. You would then be paying taxes on money you no longer have.

Fortunately, the Roth rules offer an escape hatch. Should the above situation arise, simply reverse your conversion back to a traditional IRA, and then reconvert the now smaller amount back to a new Roth. This tactic can save you thousands of dollars, but be aware that regulations permit only one such re-conversion this year.

15. Removing Roth money.

Unlike the rigid withdrawal schedules for traditional IRAs, Roths do not require you to start removing money when you reach any particular age. The funds can stay there until you die. Your unspent Roth money will then belong to your beneficiaries and—depending on who they are—can continue to grow tax-free. Be aware, though, that if your beneficiary is anyone other than your spouse, he or she will have to comply with some minimum-distribution requirement.

16. Should you convert?

The advantages of a Roth are compelling, but the account is not for everyone. To determine if it's right for you, you need to explore several questions, even though some of the answers will be little more than intelligent guesses about the future.

For example, you might be better off with a traditional account if you expect your tax bracket to drop once you stop working. In making the Roth/traditional determination, plug in variables, such as the age at which you expect to stop working, that can change the answer.

17. Nondeductible traditional IRAs.

Even if your AGI is too high to permit you to open a traditional IRA or a Roth, you can still stash a nondeductible $2,000 a year ($4,000 for a couple) in a traditional IRA. The money you earn on such contributions will accumulate tax-free until withdrawals start, at which point it will be taxed as ordinary income. Contributions made in nondeductible, after-tax dollars will not be taxed upon withdrawal, but the law treats all withdrawals—regardless of where the money originally came from—as having come proportionately from deductible and nondeductible contributions. The good news? If your AGI drops below $100,000 in any given year, you can move money out of the nondeductible account and into a conversion Roth.

18. The nightmare of Form 8606.

As you might imagine, calculating taxes on withdrawals gets very complicated. To make matters worse, you will have to file an IRS Form 8606 every year in which you make a nondeductible contribution or withdraw money from an IRA to which nondeductible contributions have been made. This form will become very familiar to you because you'll also have to fill it out for any year in which you:

- Convert part or all of the assets in a traditional IRA to a Roth IRA or the reverse;
- Receive distributions from a Roth IRA; or
- Receive distributions from a traditional IRA, if you have ever made a nondeductible contribution to any of your traditional IRAs. Translation: Hang on to the 8606 forms until you completely remove the money from all of your traditional IRAs, a process that could take decades.

19. Penalty for noncompliance.

To really twist the knife, the law authorizes the IRS to exact a $50 penalty if you do not file a required Form 8606, unless you are able to prove that the failure was due to reasonable cause. "Formophobia" does not suffice.

20. IRAs and estate taxes.

Confusion abounds about the interplay of income taxes and estate taxes. For estate-tax purposes, all IRA funds, whether housed in traditional or Roth accounts, count as part of your taxable estate, subject, at your death, to taxes of up to 55 percent.

Fortunately, the ceiling on the amount of money you can pass on to your beneficiaries before these taxes kick in is rising. Spouses can receive an unlimited amount of assets, and other beneficiaries can inherit up to $675,000 this year (and next) before they have to give the government a cut. By 2006, the ceiling will have been raised to $1 million, and there is a lot of support in Congress for both accelerating this schedule and raising the exemption amount. Stay tuned.

IF WE CAN'T TAKE IT WITH US, WE'RE SURE NOT GONNA LET THE GOVERNMENT HAVE IT!

401(k) Plans

401(k) plans have become enormously popular. In fact, according to a March, 2000 *Money* magazine article by Penelope Wang entitled "The Biggest Retirement

Decision You'll Make," up to ten percent of 401(k) owners will hold $1million or more in their accounts within the next ten years.

You can defer paying taxes on a portion of your salary by contributing it to a special account set up by your employer called a 401(k) plan. Tax isn't due on the money until it's withdrawn, usually at retirement. Companies often impose a ceiling on contributions, and the government sets another limit. Employers often chip in—typically 50 cents for every dollar you deposit

The rules for distribution of 401(k)s are similar to those for IRAs: you can withdraw funds without penalty after age 59.5 or at retirement, and you must start withdrawing by age 70.5.

Employee Savings Plans

Employee savings plans are similar to 401(k) plans, except that you deposit after-tax dollars instead of pre-tax dollars to your special account.

Employee Stock-Ownership Plans (ESOP)

Many companies have implemented employee stock-ownership plans. Indeed, MicroSoft employees became millionaires because of this type of plan. A company, through a trust it establishes, purchases shares of its own stock for employees. The trust holds the stock in individual employee accounts and distributes it to workers. You may not have to pay tax on them until you receive a distribution from the trust, typically at retirement when your tax rate may be lower.

HEAR ABOUT LEONARD? THAT SOFTWARE COMPANY HE WORKS FOR PAID HIM IN STOCK. HE'S BUYING A YACHT NEXT MONTH WHEN HE REITRES. HE'S GONNA SAIL AROUND THE WORLD!

The Ballad of Bill and Betty Continues…

Bill and Betty decided that they needed to see in black and white where they stood financially if they were to ever have a chance at accomplishing the goals they'd set way back when. So they sat down and figured out where they stood.

First off, on the plus side, they had saved about $100,000 to pay for at least part of their children's college expenses, and they were determined not to touch it. They figured they had a little over $25,000 in their savings account, although that was being eaten away, it seemed, with unexpected expenses—mostly, it seemed to Bill, Sr., on auto repair bills for Bill, Jr.'s lemon of a car. Bill's company 401(k) plan had accumulated about $250,000, although the value of the stock had been, since his company was purchased by an unscrupulous mother company and the news of their misdeeds had broken, dropping like a rock. They had roughly $25,000 in stable blue chip stocks, a house worth probably $175,000, and miscellaneous assets worth about $35,000.

On the negative side, they had about $150,000 in student loans to repay. And now Nellie's wedding, another $35,000, they figured.

As for their month-to-month obligations, Bill's salary covered that, usually with a couple of hundred dollars left over to put into their savings account for a rainy day.

With such an overview of their finances, it became clear to them that they needed to get a tighter reign on their financial situation.

CHAPTER FIVE

Only the little people pay taxes.

—Leona Helmsley

MANAGING YOUR ROLLOVER AS YOU APPROACH AND ENTER INTO RETIREMENT

In order to get the most out of your employee plan, there are a few things you should know. In a best-case scenario, a lump-sum distribution should be converted into an IRA as you approach retirement. However, this can be extremely complicated, and most employers offer little or no help or advice. Internal Revenue Service rules governing IRA rollovers alone is 70 pages long. Managing your rollover as you approach retirement can be the single most important financial decision you'll make—and one you may want to have a professional help you with.

The one universal rule is that you should draw first from your taxable accounts, so that your IRAs and 401(k)s can compound tax deferred as long as possible.

Following are some helpful guidelines to help you understand the issues involved in managing your rollover as retirement approaches.

To avoid paying an early withdrawal penalty on an IRA, take periodic payments based on your life expectancy or the joint life expectancy of you and your beneficiary.

Approaching retirement

First off, if you're older than 59 and a half and retiring, there's little reason to stick with your 401(k). Many company savings plans simply aren't that accommodating to retirees, and some plans force workers to take out all their money by the official retirement age, typically 65. If you don't make prior arrangements, such as a direct rollover into an IRA, you could be automatically mailed a check for the distribution—minus the 20 percent withholding tax.

I DON'T KNOW WHAT HAPPENED. I WAS GOING TO ROLL MY 401(K) OVER INTO AN IRA. BUT BEFORE I KNEW IT, THEY SENT ME A CHECK—AND IT WASN'T NEARLY A BIG AS IT WAS SUPPOSED TO BE.

If you really need to make withdrawals from your nest egg before age 59 and a half, an IRA rollover works well when utilizing the IRC(t). To avoid paying an early withdrawal penalty on an IRA, take periodic payments based on your life expectancy or the joint life expectancy of you and your beneficiary. (This rule for determining payment schedules applies to all IRA owners regardless of age.) The rules, which are laid out in section 72(t) of the tax code, are not that complicated. Once you start taking withdrawals, you must continue for at least five years or until you turn 59 and a half, whichever is later.

If you own a big helping of company shares in your retirement plan and you can't touch your company stock while you're still working, use an IRA rollover as an opportunity to diversify. (Most advisors suggest keeping no more than five percent of your portfolio in a single company's stock.)

Retirement

So you're no longer working. If you haven't already rolled out of your former company's 401(k) plan, think about doing that now. Most 401(k) plans that I've encountered typically offer more aggressive options than you'd probably want to consider for retirement income purposes. In general, IRAs offer the widest investment option for keeping your portfolio on track, as well as the best alternatives for distributions and estate planning. There are some things you need to consider.

If you have a nice large nest egg, you'll need to be diversified among stocks, funds and other assets. An IRA rollover offers more choice than the typical 401(k) plan. Keep in mind, however, that even though you may be changing your account, don't assume that all of the sudden you need to make major changes in your asset allocation. If you were allocating 70-100 percent of your portfolio to equities during your working years, you may do best to keep your portfolio unchanged for now. Later, you can shift more money to less volatile assets such as bonds

In general, IRAs offer the widest investment option for keeping your portfolio on track, as well as the best alternatives for distributions and estate planning.

or cash. Many retirees use stocks as the cornerstone of their strategy.

If you want to pass money on to your heirs, IRAs are the more flexible choice. Nearly all the 401(k) plans require that your spouse be listed as the primary beneficiary of your account, unless he or she signs a waiver. Major brokerage and mutual fund firms, however, generally offer plenty of beneficiary options on IRAs. (If yours doesn't, attach a customized form that spells out your wishes—or move your money to a firm that offers more flexibility.)

When it comes to mandatory withdrawals, IRAs are the way to go since they offer more options than company plans do for setting withdrawal schedules. Keep in mind, though, that by April 1 of the year following the year you turn 70 and a half, you must begin withdrawing the required minimum distributions from your tax-deferred accounts, whether they're IRAs or 401(k)s. The federal penalty for not taking out at least the minimum is stiff: a full 50 percent of the amount you should have withdrawn. And keep in mind that you are the one responsible for figuring out the number, and calculating the precise amount of that minimum distribution is not easy since the rates are based on your life expectancy and that of others you've named as beneficiaries to your account.

And finally, the last thing you should consider is getting expert advice. Indeed, the rules and regulations governing distributions and contributions and taxes are complicated and ever-changing. A good financial advisor may be able to save you hundreds of dollars. And if you have a sizable nest egg ready to be rolled over, he or she may be able to save you thousands of dollars.

The rules and regulations governing distributions and contributions and taxes are complicated and ever-changing.

The Ballad of Bill and Betty Continues...

As part of their strategy of getting a tighter reign on their finances, Bill and Betty decided to take some action on their own. Because of his company's precarious situation with pending legal action that had already adversely effected the value of the stock in his 401(k) which had performed very well over the years—legal action that could potentially even put them out of business—Bill decided to roll his 401(k) plan over into an IRA. Doing so, he reasoned, would take his money out of play in any potential fines and/or settlement that his company may be subject to once the litigation is completed and a decision rendered. It would also allow them to diversify their money into more fruitful investments.

Of course there was still the matter of paying off student loans and paying for Nellie's wedding. Bill and Betty decided to withdraw some of the money from their IRA to pay off these debts.

Had the Boomers been better informed about traxes and penalties, they would have known that because Bill was under 59 and a half years old that, in addition to paying ordinary income taxes that they would owe an IRS early withdrawal penalty of ten percent. They could have taken periodic payments based on his life expectancy under the rules set forth in the IRC, section 72(t), and paid off the student loans they took out for their children within five years—the minimum period of withdrawals allowed under the rules. They can also use the money from the first two withdrawals to help pay for Nellie's wedding next year after she finishes her MBA.

CHAPTER SIX

INVESTMENT PLANNING

The ultimate result of shielding men from folly is to fill the world with fools.

—Herbert Spencer

Investing can be a frightening experience for many older Americans. Many remember the Great Depression and hardships that their family might have had to weather. For Baby Boomers, Black Monday in 1987 (when the stock market dropped 500 points) and the savings and loan failures may hold the same sort of reminders. Consequently, many older Americans invest only in the most conservative instruments, or income investments. CDs, money market accounts, government securities, and certain mutual funds fall into this category. Such a strategy may protect capital and provide income for living expenses, but it may undermine long-term financial well-being because it doesn't provide a hedge against inflation. In order to preserve purchasing power, you need to invest in growth instruments such as stocks and real estate whose values rise and fall with changes in the economy. While they may be more volatile and risky than income investments, their potential returns are higher.

HE SAYS HE'D RATHER GO TO VEGAS THAN INVEST IN ONE OF THOSE HI-TECH COMPANIES. SAYS HE DOESN'T TRUST ANY COMPANY THAT HASN'T BEEN AROUND SINCE BEFORE THE GREAT DEPRESSION....

There are innumerable scenarios and situations when it comes to investing. My favorite rule of thumb is that there are no rules of thumb. The truth is that everyone's situation is unique and should be looked at individually. Before my clients invest I insist they implement an investment policy—a sort of roadmap to investing. This roadmap should take into consideration:

- age
- time frame until money will be needed
- what percentage of retirement income will be dependent on these monies
- and perhaps most importantly, comfort level (one should never sacrifice sleep at night for potential financial reward)

In this chapter I'll discuss some of the most common investment instruments. Again, this is only a sampling of what's out there now, and a brief summary of relevant information. As with any of the other specific elements of the Master Plan, you should supplement the information included here with your own investigations and research so that you can keep as current as possible on ever-changing options and variables.

And finally, I'll offer two philosophies for investing your retirement funds that I recommend to my clients in my own practice. These philosophies will help insure a successful retirement, getting the most out of your money without compromising your sense of security.

First off, let's examine some of the more common savings and investment instruments.

The aim of almost every investor is to obtain a combination of safety, income, and capital growth.

—John Templeton

Certificates of Deposit

Convenient, safe and easy to monitor, CDs are sold by banks and savings and loan institutions in varying denominations, typically $500 and up. Deposits up to $100,000, including any interest earned, are fully insured by the federal government.

CDs pay a higher interest rate than savings accounts but charge penalties if you withdraw the money before a fixed term, anywhere from one month to a year or more. In general, the larger the deposit and the longer the term, the higher the interest paid. Interest earned on a CD is subject to federal and state income tax. Shop around for the best deal, because interest rates vary. To save time, check the business section of your local newspaper, which may publish weekly CD rates at major banks.

If you buy more than one CD, consider staggering the terms so that you'll have cash available if you need it. A long-term CD is not the place to lock up money you may need soon.

Money Market Funds

Though considered safe, money market funds are not insured by the federal government.

Available at brokerage and investment firms, money market funds can be opened with as little as $500 and allow you to withdraw your money at any time without penalty. These funds may also offer limited check-writing privileges. Although they pay higher interest than savings accounts, their rates are generally lower than rates for CDs. Money market funds are typically invested in low-risk instruments such as government securities. Though considered safe, these funds are not insured by the federal government.

Money Market Accounts

Available at banks and savings and loans, these accounts offer investment features similar to money market funds, but with one difference: Deposits to money market accounts are insured up to $100,000 by the federal government. However, there's a catch to that extra security. Minimum deposit requirements are higher, typically $2,500 and up, and if your balance drops below that amount you'll sacrifice your high interest rate, receiving instead the rate on passbook savings accounts.

Bonds

Bonds are actually loans to the federal government, a state, local municipality, or private corporation. In return for your investment, the issuer promises to pay you a fixed rate of interest and to repay the principal after the bond matures. Generally, you can sell bonds at any time at prevailing market price, which may be higher or lower than the principal amount or the price you paid since bond prices fluctuate with the interest rate and other factors. It's a good idea to monitor your investment by checking bond prices, yields and maturity dates in a financial newspaper.

Let's examine the various types of bonds available.

U.S. Treasure Bonds

The quintessential no-risk investment, they're sold in denominations of $1,000 and up, with maturity dates ranging up to thirty years. U.S. Treasury bonds are issued by the federal government, which is extremely unlikely to default. Interest is paid every six months and is subject to federal, but not state or local income tax.

These bonds can be bought directly from the Federal Reserve banks, or from stockbrokers and commercial banks—more convenient, to be sure, but more costly as they charge a commission. Some mutual funds specialize in treasury bonds.

You can also buy shorter term treasury bills and notes. These "T-bills" are available in varying denominations, starting at $10,000, and they mature in three months to a year. Interest is paid when you buy them, typically within a week of purchase. Treasury notes are issued in denominations of $1,000 and up. They mature within two to ten years. Treasury notes pay interest semiannually.

Municipal Bonds

Purchased through stockbrokers, these bonds are IOUs issued in varying denominations by states, cities, counties, and even school districts. Since 1986, new issues of these

If you aren't willing to own a stock for 10 years, don't even think about owning it for 10 minutes.

—Warren Buffet

bonds have been severely limited, but older ones are still plentiful. They are particularly attractive to investors in higher tax brackets because they're exempt from federal, and often state and local, income taxes. Although yields on municipal bonds are comparatively low, their tax advantages usually make up for the difference.

Municipal bonds are only as good as the issuer's ability to repay them. Consequently, quality is an important criterion for selecting a municipal bond. One indicator of quality is the bond's rating, ranging from high (AAA) to low (C). Generally, the higher the rating, the lower your risk and the lower your return. Ask your stockbroker for the ratings of bonds you're considering, and exercise caution with any rated BBB or below.

Corporate Bonds

Corporations issue bonds when they want to raise money for special projects. As with municipal bonds, the quality of corporate bonds varies, so check ratings before investing. Dividends paid on corporate bonds are subject to federal, state and local income taxes.

Common and Preferred Stock

When you purchase common stock, you purchase a piece of the company that issued it. In contrast to bonds, returns on common stock are not assured; as part owner, you profit as long as the company does, a contingency partly dependent on the general economy's health and one that always carries a degree of risk. Although stocks are considered more risky than bonds, they generally outperform bonds in the long run. Ask your stockbroker about the track record of stock you're investigating. He or she can help you identify those that are more volatile.

Preferred stock is generally considered safer than common stock. Although it, too, represents part ownership in a company, it guarantees a fixed return and, in this way, resembles a bond. Also, should a company go into bankruptcy, its preferred stockholders will be paid before common stockholders.

Although stocks are considered more risky than bonds, they generally outperform bonds in the long run.

A retiree who isn't dependent on investments to produce high levels of income may feel comfortable investing a larger portion of their retirement investments in stock. For stock investments, quality companies are a good place to invest.

Mutual Funds

Mutual funds allow you to diversify your assets by pooling them with those of other small investors. The fund is professionally managed with a clearly defined investment objective. For example, one fund may aim for long-term growth of capital, while another may focus on generating current income. To achieve its goal, the fund may invest in stocks, bonds, other instruments, or a combination of all or some of the above.

Some mutual funds generate impressive returns but are they worth the risk? Funds with the highest risk-adjusted returns (sharp ratio) generate the most returns for the least amount of risk. It is very important to measure your portfolio's risk adjusted return.

Morningstar magazine is an excellent resource for most individual investors. It provides regular reviews and reporting on performance and essential statistics of mutual funds.

Annuities

Annuities are often purchased as a source of retirement income, and are available through life insurance companies. They allow you to invest money, either as a lump payment or in installments, and receive a certain sum each month for life in return.

There are two basic types of annuities:

- o variable
- o fixed

Fixed annuities can be problematic because many less reputable companies play first year/second year interest rate games.

With a variable annuity, the insurer invests your money in stocks, bonds, and other instruments whose values rise and fall with changes in the economy. Consequently, returns on variable annuities above a minimum floor specified by the insurer are not guaranteed. By contrast, a fixed annuity grows at interest rates set by the insurer. Earnings on both types of annuities accumulate on a tax-deferred basis until withdrawn.

Fixed annuities can be problematic because many less reputable companies play first year/second year interest rate games. For example, when insurance companies offer a very enticing first year rate, say nine percent, frequently half or more is actually a first year bonus. The following year, the interest rate drops to the base rate. Typically, these have very long surrender periods—ten to fifteen years, and in some cases, indefinitely—for the unsuspecting consumer.

In addition, the asset of the fixed annuity becomes the property of the insurance company. That means that if the insurance company becomes insolvent, the consumer's money is in jeopardy.

Unfortunately there are many hucksters pitching these high commission consumer traps. These products are not governed by the Securities Exchange Commission since they're not a security. So beware.

As with either a fixed or variable annuity, investing in an A-plus-rated (or better) company is almost always the best way to go. And always read the fine print.

As with either a fixed or variable annuity, investing in an A-plus-rated (or better) company is almost always the best way to go.

Variable annuities are preferable for a number of reasons—first and foremost, because the deposit does not become the property of the insurance company because it is invested in what's called a separate account.

Other benefits include:

- multiple asset classes
- no-cost transfers between funds
- multiple managers which sometimes includes institutional managers that would otherwise only be available to the very wealthy and pensions
- tax deferred growth for non-IRA accounts (Tax deferral doesn't benefit IRAs since they are already tax-deferred; however it's important to note that there is no cost for tax deferral.)
- guaranteed death benefit (Should the market be down at the time of the owners death, the beneficiary would receive no less than the original investment, and probably more, depending on the contract.)
- no sales charge—100 percent of the investment gets invested
- short surrender periods (Some policies have surrender periods of seven years or longer. I prefer those with three years or less. Surrender periods are waived if they exist at time of death and, some times, should money be needed for nursing home care.)
- avoids probate

- o can provide some protection form Medicaid spend down
- o controlled distribution

One myth is that one must annuitize an annuity to receive income, but this is simply not true. My clients receive predictable monthly income through a monthly withdrawal plan without ever annuitizing their contract.

In fact, there are a number of media myths that have needlessly scared people from considering the many benefits of a variable annuity. This particular segment of the financial market is huge—over $100 billion a year. Following are some answers and/or replies to some common objections to variable annuities.

One myth is that one must annuitize an annuity to receive income, but this is simply not true.

Annuity fees are too high.

- o Many people feel that the additional 0.6 percent per year is money well spent because it buys them tax-deferred growth, downside protection for their family, and income they can't outlive.
- o Annuities are a little more expensive than mutual funds, about 0.6 percent per year on average, compared to no-load funds. However, when you compare investment performance after expenses over the last one, three, five and ten years, variable annuities actually perform better than mutual funds, according to *Morningstar* magazine.
- o When you compare tax-deferred growth, including fees, to taxable investment, tax-deferred growth still offers a better return.
- o I can provide my clients all the benefits of an annuity for about the same cost as a B-share mutual fund.

(According to *Morningstar*, the average B-share growth mutual fund annual expense is 2.03 percent.)

Annuities under-perform mutual funds because fees are too high.

- Each year, *Morningstar* compares the total returns of over 4,000 variable annuity sub-accounts to over 6,000 equity mutual funds. Each year the findings are the same: net of fees, the variable annuity equity sub-accounts outperform the equity mutual funds over a one-, three-, five- and ten-year period.

Why should I convert capital gains to ordinary income?

- If your holding period is 7-10 years or greater, you'll end up with more money to spend, even after paying taxes at normal rates, than with an investment that's currently taxable.
- The long-term advantages of tax-deferred accumulation can far outweigh the increased rate of taxation when money is withdrawn. You'll have more money after taxes.
- Because you pay taxes every year on capital gains whether you like it or not, based on the 1099 you receive each January. However, even though distributions from a variable annuity are taxed at ordinary rates, you won't pay any taxes until you take distributions. This could be 10, 15 or 20 years!

If tax deferral doesn't make any sense, why is there so much money in IRAs and 401(k)s?

Much of the taxable income of all taxpayers in the 28 percent bracket is taxed as low as 15 percent.

- Currently equity mutual funds have an average turnover ratio of 86. This indicates that 86 percent of the stocks held in the average equity mutual fund are sold in any given year generating short-term capital gains and taxed as ordinary income.
- Although most investors will fall into the 28 percent marginal tax bracket at retirement, this does not mean, however, that they will pay taxes on annuity distributions at a 28 percent effective rate. Much of the taxable income of all taxpayers in the 28 percent bracket is taxed as low as 15 percent. For example, for 1999, a couple filing a joint return have a gross income of $115,700 resulting after deductions in a combined taxable income of $101,300. They are in the 28 percent marginal tax bracket. Of their retirement income, assume $55,000 is a taxable withdrawal from a variable annuity. Their tax burden would be: 15 percent on the first $43,050 and 28 percent on the next $58,250 = $22,767.50 = an effective tax rate of 20 percent of their gross income. Therefore it probably does not make good economic sense to pay 20 percent or more annually in income taxes on a mutual fund portfolio.

You should never own an annuity in an IRA.

- Seems like many ill-informed journalists think that you should never own an annuity in an IRA just because an annuity is already tax-deferred. It's true that there are no additional tax advantages. However, what is often overlooked is the fact that there are no additional fees for the tax deferral. One needs to consider the other benefits (let's not forget results) when determining the best investment to use—no different than when considering mutual funds. Some of the largest retirement funds in the country are annuities.

- Annuities offer much more than just tax deferral—they can provide downside protection for your family or beneficiaries, and allow you and your family to seek higher returns without the risk of loss of principal for your heirs.
- You insure your home, your car, your income and your life—why not insure your retirement?
- You can buy an annuity with no sales charge, get guaranteed downside protection, and have guaranteed income for life.

Annuities offer much more than just tax deferral—they can provide downside protection for your family or beneficiaries, and allow you and your family to seek higher returns without the risk of loss of principal for your heirs.

If my client dies, he won't get a step up in basis like a mutual fund.

- Neither will his IRA or 401(k), but they have something that the mutual fund doesn't have—a deduction for the beneficiary for the estate taxes paid on the ordinary gain. This could even the score for the beneficiary.
- In most cases the power of tax deferral over the years will not only result in more income to the owner during their life, but to the heirs as well, even taking into consideration the stepped up basis at death.

Jane Bryant Quinn says that I would be better off in an index fund.

Variable annuities offer the benefit of tax-free exchanges. Mutual funds do not.

- She gets paid to sell magazines, not help real people achieve their lifetime goals. Most columnists like her have a natural prejudice against any fund of variable annuity bought through a financial advisor. It lessens her power and ultimate readership and therefore her income. That is the equivalent to reading a medical journal to heal your sickness instead of going to the doctor.

Aren't I better off with a tax efficient mutual fund?

- In most cases no. Mutual fund proponents compare their funds with variable annuities as if the owners of the funds and annuities never make any changes to the mix.
- Variable annuities offer the benefit of tax-free exchanges. Mutual funds do not. Studies indicate that many investors switch in and out of different asset classes over the life of their investment due to changing economic and market conditions. They also frequently begin to reduce their exposure as they get older, changing from more aggressive funds to more conservative growth/income funds that will generate a taxable event(s). Also, these types of funds, particularly the balanced and income funds frequently held by retirees, typically generate much more ordinary income than capital gains.
- Section 1035 of the IRS also allows you to switch from one variable annuity to another without incurring

taxes. The inability of a mutual fund owner to obtain similar tax treatment can be costly in the real world.

- Any manager that manages mutual fund money as well as tax deferred money will tell you that their tax deferred funds will perform better over time. The decisions of when to buy and sell should be based on the fundamentals of the market and not on waiting a few more months (often at great risk) to qualify for long term gains. This gives the tax-deferred fund a tremendous advantage. The increasing volatility of the markets and the increasing pressure for the mutual fund manager to generate higher "after tax returns" over the last few years can only widen the performance advantage currently enjoyed by tax deferred funds over taxable funds.

What about Social Security taxes?

- This again favors the annuities. Social Security income recipients are subject to having from 50 to as much as 85 percent of their income taxed. A mutual fund owner could receive dividends or capital gains distributions on his/her funds that he/she doesn't currently need, thereby pushing him/her into a higher income range which could result in Social Security being 50-85 percent taxable. With a variable annuity, he/she can let the money grow tax deferred—no 1099 would be generated. Variable annuities have been used very effectively to further lower taxes to retirees by reducing the amount of Social Security income subject to taxation (an extremely sensitive issue with most retirees).

Social Security income recipients are subject to having from 50 to as much as 85 percent of their income taxed.

What about future changes in the tax laws?

- Again, this favors variable annuities. Congress' habit of changing the tax system on a fairly regular basis would be a good arguement by itself for tax deferral over "pay as you go" tax with mutual funds. The trend is towards simplifying the tax code with a flat tax, or perhaps a national sales tax or a combination of the two. Most certainly if this occurs, the overall tax rates will come down.

Congress' habit of changing the tax system on a fairly regular basis would be a good arguement by itself for tax deferral over "pay as you go" tax with mutual funds.

This would be a huge windfall for the variable annuity investor. On the other hand, a mutual fund owner may well question whether it was worth paying 20 percent or more in taxes on fund holdings over the years only to find himself in a lower tax bracket at retirement—especially if his neighbor who deferred all income taxes for years with variable annuities winds up in the same flat tax bracket.

All that said, the down-side of annuities are that, if you turn in the annuity for cash early, you'll be subject to steep surrender charges that gradually diminish each year until they disappear, typically after five to six years. As with IRAs, if you withdraw sums before you reach age 59 and a half, you'll have to pay a 10 percent penalty, plus any tax owed on the income.

You should request a prospectus for each annuity you're investigating to determine surrender fees, sales commissions, management charges, and other expenses.

Real Estate

Your most valuable investment may be one that you bought decades ago: your house. Over the years, it has probably appreciated in value at the same time that it has been providing you with a substantial tax write-off. In addition, the equity you've built in your home can be used to secure a loan or provide income in retirement. How you manage this important asset can profoundly affect your financial future.

Now that you're familiar with the most common savings and investment instruments, it wouldn't hurt to become familiar with some dos and don'ts....

WE WILL *NOT* SELL THE HOUSE AND BUY A NEW CONDO JUST SO YOU DON'T HAVE TO MOW THE LAWN!

Dos and Don'ts for Investors

What should you do?

- o Invest with a purpose, keeping your financial goals in mind.
- o Research investments adequately and obtain sound financial advice before acting.
- o As a general rule, choose investments with low or no sales charges and a history of low expense fees.
- o Deal only with reputable investment firms or financial advisors that you've had an opportunity to visit in person. Contact your local securities authority to find out whether the firm is registered to sell investments in your state. Also, call the BBB to find out whether other consumers have complained about the company.
- o Avoid any deals promising unusually high returns with no risk. If it sounds too good to be true, it almost certainly is.
- o Be wary of investments marketed by phone. The Federal Trade Commission says about three-quarters of fraudulent investment schemes are pitched by telephone.
- o Report unscrupulous salespersons to the BBB and to your state securities office.
- o Make sure you develop your own investment policy prior to investing a dime (including your company 401(k) plan).

What shouldn't you do?

- o Don't think you retire on a lump sum of money; you retire on the income that the lump sum of money generates,

- Don't invest in instruments you don't understand, even if a reputable advisor recommends them.
- Don't put all your eggs in one basket. Diversify your investments to spread your risk.
- Don't assume more risk than you can comfortably tolerate. If an investment is keeping you awake at night, it's time to unload it—or at the very least, diversify.
- Don't let tax considerations drive your investments. Remember that tax laws are subject to change. Your foremost considerations should be what you can afford and your financial goals.
- Don't use long-term investments to solve short-term financial problems.
- Don't shuffle investments in response to hot trends and tips. Stay focused on your true investment goals.

- o Don't give financial advisors authority to invest your assets without your approval of each transaction.
- o Don't pay cash for an investment.

One of the most frequent mistakes I see with investors in general is a lack of understanding of how investments work. The following questions will help you understand how an investment will work for you:

How liquid is it?

Liquidity refers to the ease with which an investment can be converted into its market value. Savings—very liquid. Home—not so much. There's no rule, but keep in mind that you'll need enough income to meet short-term obligations.

How risky is it?

Generally, the more risk you assume, the more you stand to gain. At the same time, of course, the more you stand to lose. Assess your own tolerance for risk.

What is its yield?

Yield is a measure of the investment's performance. It may be fixed and assured (CDs), or it may fluctuate over time (stocks).

There are three philosophies for investing your retirement funds that have proven useful in helping insure a successful retirement without compromising the sense of security that should be part and parcel of any responsible retirement strategy:

1) evaluate your income needs and support that income with fixed income securities;

2) consider investing in quality (blue chip) stocks or funds to help you keep up with future inflation which will surely effect your future lifestyle;

3) review your portfolio at least annually; as economics change, so must your investments—but always keep in mind that they should always fit into your investment policy.

One of the most often overlooked elements of a successful retirement strategy is the emotional/psychological aspect of making your money work for you.

Every person's situation is unique and special—and not just because of the amount of money that they have. One of the most often overlooked elements of a successful retirement strategy is the emotional/psychological aspect of making your money work for you. Too often, retirees are goaded into strategies that they're uncomfortable with because an over-zealous advisor "sells" them on the idea that it has worked wonders and miracles for other clients. Never be afraid to tell your planner or advisor that you're not other clients, and that you have been doing something a certain way and it has worked very nicely for you, both in terms of financial reward, and peace of mind. Remember, a happy, fulfilling retirement is the goal; not beating the average or median, or competing with your peers.

The Ballad of Bill and Betty Continues….

One warm summer evening as the turn of the century approached, Bill and Betty were watching a news magazine program on TV about all the millionaires that were made in the hi-tech/dot-com craze in the last decade of the 20th century. Bill had never been much of a gambler.

In fact, he'd never even placed a bet at a blackjack table or stuck a coin in a slot machine. Nevertheless, the temptation was too great. Bill decided to invest a portion of their savings in some high-risk hi-tech stocks.

Had he taken more time to study the market and the dynamics of the hi-tech/dot-com phenomenon, he would have discovered that it is on the wane, and that the media hype that still exists is more concerned with getting viewers to tune in or buy the magazine than with informed reporting. Indeed, much of the media hype on any given economic matter is little more than self-fulfilling political rhetoric or glamorous ad copy. One can be extremely tempted to invest in high roller investments, like dot-com companies, due to peer pressure, media hype, impatience or just plain greed.

The truth of the matter is that Bill shouldn't invest more than he is willing to lose. In some ways, investing in hi-tech/dot-com companies is very much like going to Las Vegas. This is not the time in his life to get stupid and impatient.

Perhaps Will Rogers said it best: "I'm more interested in the return *of* my money than the return *on* my money."

CHAPTER SEVEN

ISSUES AND TOPICS IN FINANCIAL PLANNING

In this world, nothing can be said to be certain except death and taxes.

—Benjamin Franklin

Income Tax Planning

According to the IRS, about half of Americans over the age of 65 do not owe federal income tax. The Senate Special Committee on Aging cites three provisions in the tax code that are significant to older adults:

1) the exclusion of veterans' pension income and, for single persons with adjusted gross incomes less than $25,000 ($32,000 for couples filing jointly), the exclusion of Social Security and railroad retirement benefits from taxation;

2) the exclusion of up to $250,000 ($500,000 for couples) in capital gains from the sale of a home (you are required to have lived in the property for at least two out of the last five years);

3) the elderly tax credit for low-income persons with few or no Social Security benefits.

The downside of this is that older folks who do pay federal income tax tend to pay at a higher rate than other age groups. According to the Senate Special Committee on Aging, the effective tax rate for older taxpayers was 17 percent, compared to 14 percent for other taxpayers.

According to the Senate Special Committee on Aging, the effective tax rate for older taxpayers was 17 percent, compared to 14 percent for other taxpayers.

What can one do to ease the tax burden? Seek professional help—especially if you have a high income or unusually complicated tax situation. The American Association of Retired Persons (AARP) advises that you should ask the following questions when interviewing potential tax advisors:

1) Are you open all year long, or only at tax time?

2) What will you charge to handle my taxes?

3) What is your professional and educational back ground?

4) Will you accompany me to the IRS if I am audited? What is the additional cost of this service?

5) Will I get a refund from the IRS?

6) Will you provide references from people in financial or business situations similar to my own?

If you don't have to itemize deductions and have few tax problems, free tax assistance programs may be the best way to go.

Insurance Planning

The first thing you should ask yourself is whether you really need life insurance. If your children are self-supporting and your spouse would have sufficient income if you died, you may not need life insurance. Of course, you may want to purchase life insurance so that loved ones are well-taken care of should you die. However, if you contribute to the financial well-being of others, you probably do need coverage.

Consumer Reports recommends a three-step approach to calculate a dollar-amount of the insurance you might need:

1) determine your family's expenses

2) analyze your assets and sources of income that you can use to cover your expenses

If your children are self-supporting and your spouse would have sufficient income if you died, you may not need life insurance.

3) subtract the assets from the needs

The result is the amount of additional insurance you need to buy. Often overlooked, however, is income requirements. Will any income need to be replaced? Addressing this issue concisely is difficult. A rough guideline, however, might be that for every $700 per month worth of income needed, an additional $100,000 in funds is needed.

The next thing you need to do is determine what type of policy is best for you. Essentially, there are five basic types of life insurance:

1) term life
2) whole life
3) universal life
4) variable life
5) variable-universal life

Some of these combine life insurance with a tax-deferred savings plan. These types of policies can be a good way for people who need the death benefits to save for retirement. However, the *Wall Street Journal* cautions that insurance works as a retirement investment only if premiums are paid for many years. Further, financial advisors caution that insurance is more complex—and often less rewarding as an investment—than it first appears.

Before you buy a life insurance policy, make sure you understand it and have shopped around for the best deal. Ask about free-look provisions which allow you approximately ten days to examine the policy, with the option of returning it for a refund if you're not satisfied.

Following are the most common types of life insurance, and a brief description of each:

Term Life Insurance

Term life insurance policies provide coverage for a limited number of years and pay benefits in the event of death. They do not, however, build up a cash value. Each dollar spent is used to buy coverage, so at first these policies provide the largest death benefit for your insurance dollar. But as you grow older, premiums jump in proportion to benefits. Most term life policies cannot be renewed beyond a certain age—usually 65 or 70. After that, you'll have to buy or convert to another type of policy. If you buy a term life policy with a conversion clause, make sure you understand the conditions that will be imposed.

Whole Life Insurance

Often referred to as straight or ordinary life, these policies combine life insurance with a savings account that accumulates a cash value on a tax-deferred basis. They offer coverage for as long as you live, regardless of your health or age, with no increase in premiums. Although premiums are initially higher than those for term insurance, they're comparatively cheaper as you grow older.

The cash value accrued in the later years of your policy can be used to supplement retirement income since you can borrow money from the policy at an interest rate specified in the policy. Any money you owe at the time of your death is deducted from the policy's benefits.

If you surrender a whole life policy soon after purchase, your return will be sharply reduced by agents' commissions. These charges decline each year until they vanish, typically after five to ten years.

Universal Life Insurance

A more flexible version of whole life, these policies allow you to modify the amount and timing of premium payments and control your cash-value growth. Your death benefits may also rise and fall, but they will never fall below a guaranteed minimum. As with whole life policies, universal life policies are considered poor buys if surrendered early.

Variable Life Insurance

Although these policies accumulate cash value, you (not the insurer) decide how to invest your premiums. Your death benefit and cash value may go up or down, depending upon how your investments perform. Consequently, these can be particularly risky buys for novice investors. As with whole life insurance, you pay a fixed premium. Cash value policies, however, can be good tools for transferring wealth to heirs since the death benefit is free from state and federal income tax. Death benefits may also be free from estate taxes if your estate is smaller or if the policy is owned by an irrevocable life insurance trust.

Variable-Universal Life Insurance

A combination of variable and universal life policies, they allow you to vary your premium payments and death benefit and to choose your own investments. Again, novice investors should be careful with these policies.

Since for many retirees the issue of insurance is such a problematic area, I'll discuss it in greater detail in Chapter Eight.

Estate Planning

Part of retirement planning is securing the well-being of those you love. Procrastination is the biggest problem most people have with this particular area of financial planning. Nobody likes to think about dying.

Estate planning is the process of setting forth binding instructions so that when you die, your personal property and other assets are distributed according to your wishes, and with a minimum of bother and expense for your heirs. I suggest, however, that estate planning is not about death; it's about life. It allows you to pass on a part of your life for the care of others. Think of it as a final act of love.

The first thing you need to do is calculate your net worth. You can use the Net Worth Worksheet in Chapter Three. Remember that the legal documents you select for distributing your estate will depend, in part, on your net worth, so it's important to be as accurate as possible.

After you've calculated your net worth, don't forget to project the future value of what your estate may be worth when you are more likely to die. (My web site, www.myplanningpartner.com, has a good estate calculator that you can use.) Then find out what the estate tax rules are so you can take steps to minimize these taxes if necessary. In some cases—specifically, if your net worth exceeds $675,000—your best strategy for reducing estate tax is to seek advice from an estate attorney or a qualified estate advisor.

Now let's take a look at some of the tools for distributing your assets that are available.

YOUR WILL

For many people, a will constitutes the foundation of their estate plan. Your will designates how and to whom your assets will be distributed when you die. It also allows you to name an executor to carry out the terms of your will and to appoint a guardian for any dependent children. It allows your heirs to settle your estate more easily, and can save money in taxes and other settlement expenses.

LIVING TRUSTS

A living trust avoids a complex probate proceeding; allows quick distribution to your heirs; eliminates probate fees and costs, and saves substantial death taxes. To create a living trust, you transfer title to real estate, stocks, bonds, bank accounts, and other assets to a trust while you're still alive. You also designate a trustee who is responsible for managing your assets.

Trust documents also allow you to name a successor trustee, who steps in to manage and distribute your assets after you die or should you become incapacitated. If you set up a revocable living trust, you can change it at any time. An irrevocable living-trust cannot be altered unless the court determines that its provisions are unworkable or that they frustrate the trust's general purpose. Unlike wills, living trusts do not go through probate; thus, your estate may be settled faster and with less expense.

However there are disadvantages to a living trust. Transferring titles to homes, bank accounts, and business and other investments into the name of the trust can be cumbersome and time-consuming. When refinancing a home, some lenders require that the house title be taken out of a trust, although it can be placed back in afterward.

Also, the legal fees for setting up a living trust tend to be substantially higher than they are for preparing a will.

For these reasons, living trusts may not be the best option for people with few assets.

Testamentary Trusts

A testamentary trust is created by your will and becomes effective after you die. They offer many of the same tax-avoidance advantages of living trusts, however they must go through probate.

Joint Tenancy

In the most common type of joint ownership, joint tenancy with a right of survivorship, two persons own property—such as real estate, bank accounts, or investments—in both names. When one co-tenant dies, the other becomes sole owner of the entire property. The surviving tenant is entitled to the property without probate. Keep in mind that you or your co-tenant may have a parting of the ways, and your property may be sold out from under you.

Another drawback is that if a parent puts a child on the deed as joint tenant, the property becomes subject to attachment for the debts of the child. Also, the first joint tenant to die cannot dispose of the property under his or her will, and the surviving tenant is under no legal obligations to share the property with other heirs. Because of these factors, it's best to seek legal advice before placing large assets under joint tenancy.

A living trust avoids a complex probate proceeding; allows quick distribution to your heirs; eliminates probate fees and costs, and saves substantial death taxes.

LETTER OF LAST INSTRUCTION

You can facilitate the transfer of property to your heirs by preparing a letter of last instruction to be opened at death.

HE SAYS THERE'S A SURPRISE
WAITING FOR US ALL WHEN HE DIES....

The letter should include the location of:

- o your will or trust instructions
- o birth and marriage certificates
- o insurance policies
- o bank passbooks and numbers
- o proof of ownership or property, checking accounts, credit cards, cars, houses, stocks, retirement benefits

All the same, sir, I would put some of the colonies in your wife's name.

—Joseph Herman Hertz

Regardless of the size of your estate, proper planning should be considered. While your estate may not be all that large now, it could easily double or triple during retirement, thus making it very difficult to protect your estate if you will your share to your spouse.

Another consideration is how you want your estate distributed. Do you want your estate to go directly to your kids? This way could allow your estate to enter your children's marital property. Should there be a divorce, your ex-son-in-law or daughter-in-law has the chance to walk away with a chunk of your estate.

Or do you like the idea of your estate to stay in your bloodline and go to your grandchildren should there be any money left after the death of your children? Or how about the future spouse? Had Barbara remarried, there would have been a good chance that, had she died before her new spouse, the estate could have passed on to her new spouse and his children.

It's best to seek legal advice before placing large assets under joint tenancy.

I could go on and on with different examples and scenarios. The point I'd like to make is that one doesn't have to have a large estate to benefit from good estate planning. In fact, taxes are only one part of it. If you'd like to keep your estate out of probate and control the distribution of your estate to make sure your children and grandchildren are protected from current, future or former spouses, you might want to consider the many benefits of a living trust.

Advance Directives for Protecting Your Assets

Durable Powers of Attorney

A durable power of attorney allows you to transfer as much or as little power as you want. You can authorize another person to manage your property, or simply to sell your car. You can also stipulate how long you want the power of attorney to remain in effect, and you can cancel at any time.

A durable power of attorney can be used to instruct someone to make health-care decisions on your behalf should you become disabled, including the kind and intensity of health care.

Some states restrict the use of durable powers of attorney to financial matters, so check the rules, regulations and restrictions before you execute the necessary paperwork.

Medical Directives (Living Wills)

A living will is a directive to physicians and family members that you not be given extraordinary treatment if it will only prolong your dying. In the event you are unable to express your wishes, your attending physician is legally obligated to carry out the terms of your living will.

There are severe limitations on living wills, and they vary from state to state. Most lawyers and physicians agree that a durable medical power of attorney is better.

A living will is a directive to physicians and family members that you not be given extraordinary treatment if it will only prolong your dying.

The Ballad of Bill and Betty Continues…

Bill's parents, Fred and Barbara, were always pretty smart with their money—especially when it came to looking for deals and investing. However they neglected to do proper estate planning.

Fred and Barbara had wanted for Bill and his sister Emma to receive everything that they had worked hard for. Both Bill and Emma had tried to talk to their parents about their estate planning but Fred really didn't want to listen and would tell them it was all taken care of. Fred and Barbara had prepared a simple will through one of those do-it-yourself will packages that they bought at the local business store. There was no way that Fred was going to spend a thousand or two just to have an attorney write up a few documents.

As with most folks, Fred and Barbara set each other up as beneficiaries. It seemed like the most logical thing to do. And because their estate was relatively small ($725,000), they didn't see any need for a trust.

Fred passed away about ten years ago and everything passed on to Barbara. Barbara was lost without Fred and, shortly after Fred's death, Barbara's health started failing. Barbara passed away a few months ago.

Bill and his sister Emma quickly learned that their parents' estate fell victim to the IRS. You see, Fred thought estate planning was only for the rich and famous. By making each other the beneficiaries on their policies, they lost their first unified tax exemption of $600,000 when Fred passed away. Over the next ten years, their estate more than doubled. A lot of the estate was Barbara's IRA that she had transferred to her after Fred's death.

Bill and Emma received only about $195,000 from their mother's $760,000 IRA due to federal and state income tax, and of course the estate tax. They received only 1/3 of their parents' estate after everything was said and done.

CHAPTER EIGHT

HEALTH INSURANCE: PLANNING THROUGH THE CHAOS

By the end of the 20th century, the health insurance question in the United States had reached its boiling point. The public call for health care reform combined with the medical community and insurance industry's profit motive and self interests had created a quagmire of confusion, anxiety and frustration, and a pervading sense of helplessness amongst those caught in the middle—the old and infirm, those who had been socialized to believe that they would be the beneficiaries of the system they helped establish. And despite a great public outcry for reform, political action seems no closer at the beginning of the 21st century than it was a decade before when politicians first started decrying its importance. Most experts agree that it will get worse before it gets better.

Because appropriate planning in this area can be the single most important element in your retirement planning strategy, I want to explore some of the issues involved in purchasing health insurance.

We have the wolf by the ears; and we can neither hold him, nor safely let him go. Justice is in one scale, and self-preservation in the other.

—Thomas Jefferson

[A journalist] asked, "Mr. Gandhi, what do you think of modern civilization?"

Mr. Gandhi said, "That would be a good idea."

First off, let's identify some of the most frequently asked questions:

- Should I buy long-term-care insurance? If so, what policies are best?

- I'm considering joining an HMO. How do HMOs compare with traditional insurance plans?

- Do I need private insurance to supplement Medicare? How much extra coverage will be enough?

- My wife needs nursing-home care. How can I pay her expenses and still have enough money to take care of myself?

The first issue to address is what type of plan will work best for you: Group or individual? Let's examine the specifics.

Group Plans vs. Individual Plans

Group insurance coverage costs the consumer less than comparable individual coverage. In addition, many employers who offer group health benefits subsidize the premiums so that workers pay even less for their coverage. Many group plans provide more comprehensive coverage, including benefits for extras such as dental and vision care.

If your employer, former employer, or union offers group health insurance, you should almost always enroll in the insurance plan. Generally, you get adequate coverage for hospital and medical care at comparatively low monthly premiums. If you don't have group coverage through employment, you may be eligible for group insurance through a professional association or fraternity. However, you should shop around as some association group rates are higher than those for comparable individual policies.

Medicare

If your employer, former employer, or union offers group health insurance, you should almost always enroll in the insurance plan.

When you reach 65, you will be eligible for Medicare, the nation's largest group insurance plan for older Americans, with over 33 million members nationwide. Established in 1965 as a part of LBJs Great Society, most Americans are aware of this federal health insurance program. However most Americans over the age of 45 (about 75 percent, according to a survey by the AARP) admit they know "not much" or "only some" about what Medicare covers and how much it pays in reimbursement. Knowing a little about Medicare can be worse than knowing nothing since knowing a little may lead a person to false assumptions about the program.

For instance, beneficiaries are required to pay premiums, deductibles, and coinsurance. Indeed, total out-of-pocket health costs for older people average about 15 percent of their income—the same proportion as before Medicare was enacted, according to the Senate Special Committee on Aging.

Another example of how knowing a little may be worse than knowing a lot is if you plan to keep working after 65, you have to apply for Medicare. Enrollment is automatic only for retirees.

Still yet, if you or a spouse need nursing home care, Medicare will not foot the entire bill. Many people believe that it may provide partial reimbursement in some instances. Medicare, however, defines most situations

Knowing a little about Medicare can be worse than knowing nothing, since knowing little may lead a person to false assumptions about the program.

wherein nursing home care is involved as custodial. Medicare does not pay for custodial care.

Medicare rules and regulations are not set in stone and, in fact, may change on a political whim—as it did in 1988 when Congress enacted the first major expansion of the program, and then turned right around and repealed the catastrophic care benefits in 1989.

For more detailed information about eligibility, benefits, and reimbursement, check the latest edition of *The Medicare Handbook.* You can obtain a copy at your local Social Security office, or by calling (800) 234-5772.

Enrollment in Medicare

When you turn 65, you are eligible for Medicare. Almost anyone 65 or older can enroll, but if neither you nor your spouse has accumulated enough Social Security or government work credits to be insured, you'll have to buy into the system. If you're receiving Social Security or railroad retirement benefits, you will automatically be enrolled on your 65th birthday. If you plan to keep working past 65, however, or if you have to buy into the system, you have to apply.

What Medicare covers

Medicare consists of two parts. The first, Part A (hospital insurance), covers inpatient care, skilled home-health care, hospice care, and some convalescence in a skilled nursing facility. Part B provides medical insurance and helps pay for doctor's services, outpatient procedures, diagnostic tests, durable medical equipment such as wheelchairs, and many other services and supplies not covered under Part

A. Enrollment is voluntary and requires payment of a monthly premium, but you won't find comparable benefits at a lower rate.

If you're receiving Social Security or railroad retirement benefits, you will automatically be enrolled on your 65th birthday.

Participating providers

Medicare pays 80 percent of fees that it defines as reasonable; you are responsible for the remaining 20 percent, called coinsurance. If your doctor, nursing home, or home-health agency charges more than the amount approved by Medicare, you will have to pay those charges as well as the coinsurance. Physicians are prohibited from charging more than 15 percent above the amount approved by Medicare.

One way to avoid out-of-pocket expenses is to use doctors and suppliers who have agreed to accept Medicare's approved amount as payment in full. Such doctors or suppliers can charge you only for the portion of the Part B deductible you have not met and for the coinsurance. About 40 percent of the nation's doctors accepted what is called Medicare assignment. Those who do can save you time as well as money because they submit the claim forms. For the names and addresses of participating doctors and suppliers, consult the Medicare Participating Physician/Supplier Directory, available free from your Medicare carrier.

What Medicare doesn't cover

Medicare does not cover certain kinds of care, charges, or supplies. (Most private insurance policies don't cover these items either.)

For the names and addresses of participating doctors and suppliers, consult the Medicare Participating Physician/Supplier Directory, available free from your Medicare carrier.

- private-duty nursing
- care in a skilled-nursing home after 100 days each year (skilled-nursing facilities have staff and equipment to provide round-the-clock nursing care or rehabilitation services prescribed by a doctor)
- custodial services (help in walking, getting in and out of bed, eating, and dressing), whether in a nursing facility or at home
- intermediate nursing-home care (such care may require the skills of a nurse but at a less intensive level than that given in a skilled-nursing facility)
- physician fees above Medicare's approved amount
- drugs and medicines you buy yourself, with or with out a prescription
- care received outside the U.S., except under limited circumstances in Canada and Mexico
- dental care or dentures, check-ups, most routine immunizations, cosmetic surgery, routine foot care, and examinations for and the cost of eye glasses or hearing aids

During the first half of 2000, the President insisted that congress pass a Medicare prescription drug benefit. To make a long and infuriating story short, congress rattled their sabers and proclaimed their mission noble, but couldn't agree on the elements of the legislation. By the time they were finished with business-as-usual, they did nothing.

Instead, they decided to send a bill to the President that would eliminate the so-called marriage penalty tax—a bill that would not only benefit younger Americans in a high tax bracket, but would reduce the amount of funds available to address Social Security, Medicare and Medicaid issues that are far more important and immediate. It was also a transparent political effort to lay the blame for the dead-in-the-water Medicare prescription benefit bill, as well as the doomed bill that would eliminate the marriage penalty tax at the door of the President, as he has made it all to clear that he would veto the bill unless it includes a Medicare prescription drug benefit.

Obviously, our elected officials are still unwilling to address the needs of a growing number of their constituency, and will continue to play political games with the health and well-being of older Americans in ill health and with fixed incomes. I suspect that this appalling behavior shall not soon be forgotten by the vast number of Baby Boomers on the brink of retirement.

Obviously, our elected officials are still unwilling to address the needs of a growing number of their constituency, and will continue to play political games with the health and well-being of older Americans in ill health and with fixed incomes.

Medicaid

Medicaid is the principle source for public financing of long-term care. Not only does the program spend about 40 percent of its budget on nursing-home care each year, but a majority of nursing home residents receive Medicaid assistance. Medicaid (Medi-Cal in California), like Medicare, is a government insurance program that offers basic coverage for health and medical services. Despite these shared attributes and the often confusing similarity in their names, the two programs have important differences. Medicaid is:

- administered by state governments within broad federal guidelines

- designed to provide health-care benefits to people with very low incomes and few assets

- required to cover extended stays in skilled-nursing homes and provide optional coverage for services delivered in intermediate-care facilities.

If you need extended nursing home care, one of the most prudent things you can do is to hasten the day when you qualify for Medicaid.

Even if you receive Medicare, you may be eligible for Medicaid—if not immediately, then possibly some later time if you require long-term care. If you need extended nursing home care, one of the most prudent things you can do is to hasten the day when you qualify for Medicaid.

Granted, the Medicaid program is extremely complicated. Because states have discretion in administering Medicaid, scarcely any two programs are alike. Services available, eligibility criteria, and reimbursement rates vary from state to state. The best source of up-to-date information is the state or local government department that administers the program.

Eligibility guidelines

In most states you qualify for Medicaid if you are at least 65, blind, or disabled, and you meet the eligibility standards for supplemental security income (SSI), and income support program for poor people. In 1991, a qualifying SSI applicant must have had no more than $407 a month in income and $2,000 in assets. Recipients can keep certain assets and still be eligible. Those assets include:

- o your home;
- o your personal effects and household goods worth up to $2,000;
- o your automobile (regardless of its value, as long as you need it to work or to receive medical care);
- o a burial fund of $1,500 or less.

Check with your state's program about the specifics of eligibility in your state, as there are several states with more strict eligibility standards. If you have slightly more income or assets than your state's SSI program allows, you may still qualify for some relief under Medicaid.

Fee-for-Service Plans

Known as "full-freedom-of-choice" plans because they allow you to choose your own doctor and hospital, this option comes with a price. Although their monthly premiums are often competitive with premiums in other plans, you'll pay a higher deductible and have to "co-pay" a share of covered hospital and medical expenses—usually 20 percent of each bill, up to a specified cap. In addition, you'll be responsible for any charges in excess of those deemed reasonable by the insurer. Consequently, some fee-for-service policyholders and most Medicare beneficiaries who choose this type of plan—and the vast majority still do—buy supplemental insurance policies to help defray out-of-pocket expenses.

Generally, fee-for-service policies cover hospital, surgical, and medical care, as well as ancillary services including x-rays, lab work, diagnostic tests, and drugs provided by the hospital. Limited home-health services and mental health care may also be provided, but routine physical exams and other preventive services are not.

If you choose this type of plan, either you or your doctor will have to fill out claim forms. This task can be tedious, and if forms are completed improperly, payment may be delayed.

Preferred-Provider Organizations

Essentially fee-for-service plans, preferred-provider organizations (PPOs) are groups of health-care professionals under contract with insurance companies to provide services at discounted prices. As long as you receive care from participating doctors and hospitals, your deductibles and co-payments will be lower than those of conventional fee-for-service plans. If you choose to use providers outside the system, you will still be reimbursed , but at lower rates.

PPOs provide about the same health-care benefits as full-freedom-of-choice plans. They, too, focus on acute care rather than on preventive care. However, usually there are no claim forms to complete.

Health Maintenance Organizations

Health Maintenance Organizations are composed of hospitals, doctors, and other medical personnel who serve an enrolled group for a fixed fee, paid in advance. In essence, HMOs insure you and provide your medical services as well.

For many, the lure of an HMO is the savings it offers. In return for prepaid premiums, the HMO guarantees to deliver all medically necessary services with nominal deductibles and co-payments—an advantage over fee-for-service plans. Also, because services are prepaid, there are usually no claim forms to submit.

While saving money and time, you'll also receive broader benefits. In addition to covering the basics (hospital, surgical, and medical care), HMOs offer benefits for a wide range of preventive health services, including regular physical exams, outpatient drugs and, in some cases, eyeglasses, hearing aids, and exercise programs.

In return for prepaid premiums, the HMO guarantees to deliver all medically necessary services with nominal deductibles and co-payments—an advantage over fee-for-service plans.

OF COURSE I'D LIKE TO CHOOSE MY OWN DOCTOR, BUT THE PRICE IS RIGHT....

On the other side of the coin, however, enrollees must use the HMOs physician and hospital facilities, and they may not always see the physician or specialist of their choice. This can be troublesome, particularly when you consider that many HMO health providers have only limited experience treating older patients. Fewer than five percent of HMO enrollees are 65 or older, according to the AARP.

Another major drawback is limited selection. To qualify for membership, you must live within the HMOs specified geographic region or service area. If you receive Medicare, you can only select among HMOs that have contracts with Medicare.

Also, most HMOs do not provide home-health services. And there have been a great many complaints in recent years about increasing premiums, cut benefits, and dropped Medicare beneficiaries. So it's incumbent upon you to shop carefully before joining a plan. One way to do this is to talk to people in your own age group who are current or former members of the HMO you're considering. Find out what they liked most, least, the providers, and the care they received. Visit the HMO and talk with the staff.

Choosing the best plan

The best health-care plan is in the eye of the beholder. A plan that suits a friend may not suit you. If you have a choice among plans, base your selection on a thorough consideration of each in light of your current and anticipated health needs and your budget. Ask yourself these questions:

- What type of plan would work best for me?
- What benefits do I need in a health plan?
- Is it important that I choose my own doctor and hospital?
- Can I cover out-of-pocket expenses or afford a health-insurance supplement to help defray them?
- Am I diligent about completing and submitting claim forms?

If the plan you select doesn't meet your needs, you usually can switch to another. Medicare beneficiaries and individual policy-holders can switch at any time; people covered by group insurance policies generally may change plans only during certain weeks or months of the year, when their employer or group association declares an open enrollment period.

Supplemental Insurance

There are four basic types of supplemental insurance policies:

1) Medicare supplemental policies
2) hospital-indemnity policies
3) specified disease policies
4) long-term care policies

These policies are intended to provide additional health-care benefits to basic coverage. They should never be purchased in place of broader forms of coverage. Many supplemental policies provide important health-care benefits; some offer more than they eventually plan to deliver.

Medicare supplemental insurance

Often called medigap policies, these plans are designed to help fill some of the gaps in Medicare coverage. In accordance with regulations established by the National Association of Insurance Commissioners (NAIC), every medigap policy is required to provide coverage for the following items:

- Either all of the Medicare hospital deductible or none of it. This either-or requirement makes it easier for consumers to compare Medicare supplemental insurance policies.

- The Medicare hospital coinsurance, plus 90 percent of per diem hospital expenses not covered by Medicare, up to a maximum of 365 additional days.

- The blood-transfusion deductible, unless the blood is replaced by the policyholder.

- The 20 percent co-payment for physician services, after the policyholder pays the Part B deductible.

More than the specific details, it's important to know that minimum standards apply to every Medicare supplemental-insurance policy sold in the United States. In general, you'll never need more than one medigap policy; buying two only wastes money on duplicate minimum coverage. According to a 1987 study by the Health Insurance Association of America, 5.6 million older Americans have been the victim of what consumer advocate David Horowitz calls "medicrap abuse." While the NAIC has drafted model regulations to crack down on such abuses, buyers should still beware. To help you protect yourself against fast-talking hucksters, you need to read between the lines of these commonly used, often misleading sales pitches:

According to a 1987 study by the Health Insurance Association of America, 5.6 million older Americans have been the victim of what consumer advocate David Horowitz calls "medicrap abuse."

- A social security Medicare worker comes calling to sell you a medigap policy. Don't believe it. Representatives of these federal programs don't sell or service such insurance.

- A saleswoman explains that Medicare does not cover extended stays in a nursing home, then pitches a medigap policy. Her statement is true as far as it goes: Medicare helps pay for care in a skilled-nursing facility for only 100 days and does not cover stays of any length in intermediate- or custodial-care nursing homes.

  But the agent has misled you by implying that medigap policies cover lengthy nursing-home stays. They don't. Medigap policies do not pay for custodial or intermediate care at home or in a nursing home, the type of care older persons are most likely to need for long-term illnesses. Consumers can purchase insurance policies that cover long-term care, but these are presently distinct from medigap policies and do not supplement Medicare hospital and physician benefits.

- A medigap insurance agent asks whether you'd be interested in a policy that prevents you from becoming a burden to your spouse or children. With your worst fears aroused, you have difficulty resisting the sales pitch. The implication is that medigap insurance offers coverage for long-term care. Once again, it doesn't.

  If you're worried about what will happen if you ever need extended care, discuss your concerns with family members and explore options such as purchasing long-term-care insurance or buying into a continuing-care retirement community.

- An insurance rep asks whether you'd like coverage for prescription drugs. You would, because your current medigap policy doesn't provide this benefit.

If you have group medical coverage through a current or former employer, you probably don't need supplemental insurance.

Some higher priced medigap policies provide more insurance than the law requires—for prescription drugs, physician fees in excess of Medicare-approved charges, or other benefits. Monthly premiums for these policies pay for the standard medigap insurance plus the additional coverage.

If you want broader coverage to supplement Medicare, upgrade your current medigap policy, if possible, or exchange it for one that fits your needs. (If you change policies, check for clauses on pre-existing conditions that may limit your coverage.) Don't buy an extra policy; you'll waste money duplicating insurance.

Before you buy any medigap policy, ask yourself whether you really need it. If you have group medical coverage through a current or former employer, you probably don't need supplemental insurance. Ditto for people who receive both Medicare and Medicaid (Medicare providers are required to accept the Medicaid reimbursement as payment in full), and for HMO enrollees, who incur only limited out-of-pocket expenses.

Hospital-indemnity policies

These policies pay a flat rate for each day the policyholder is in the hospital, regardless of benefits paid by other health insurance. Payments work like pocket money, to be used for whatever the recipient pleases.

Sold through agents or directly from insurance companies by mail, hospital-indemnity policies require careful shopping and close scrutiny. Because benefits are fixed, they also need periodic updating to keep pace with inflation. Some policies do not pay benefits until after a few days of hospitalization, and some pay nothing for outpatient visits. Weigh these considerations against shorter hospital stays for older patients these days and the increasing number of operations performed on an outpatient basis.

While everyone should think twice before buying a hospital-indemnity policy, some people should think thrice. HMO enrollees can probably do without this insurance because their out-of-pocket expenses are limited. Also, to the extent that these policies are designed to replace wages lost during hospitalization, you may not need one if you're living on retirement income and have adequate basic health coverage.

One common but ill-conceived practice is to buy a hospital-indemnity policy figuring you'll make money in it if you're hospitalized frequently or long enough. And you might. But if that's your idea of a good investment, then I've got a bridge I'd like to show you—and it's priced for quick sale!

Specified-disease policy

Also called dread-disease policies, these pay benefits for the treatment of a single disease, such as cancer, or a group of diseases specified in the policy. Typically, such policies are not available to people who have been previously diagnosed or treated for the specified ailment.

On a scale of one to ten, with one representing a bad guy, we give dread-disease policies a quarter of a point for

On a scale of one to ten, with one representing a bad guy, we give dread-disease policies a quarter of a point for their next-to-nothing coverage.

their next-to-nothing coverage. They're like shooting dice with the odds stacked against you.

So why do some people buy the dread-disease insurance? Often because they mistakenly believe that such coverage will protect them from the high cost of long-term care. What should they do instead? First and foremost, explore their options.

Protecting yourself against long-term-care costs

- Conservative estimates are that one in every three persons over 65 will enter a nursing home at some point in their lives.
- On average, a year in a nursing home costs between $35,000 and $50,000, according to industry experts.
- After only thirteen weeks in a nursing home, 70 percent of older persons living alone become poor; within a year, over 90 percent are impoverished, according to the U.S. House Select Committee on Aging. The outlook for married couples is only somewhat less bleak: one out of two couples become impoverished after one spouse has spent half a year in a nursing home.

Discouraging as they are, these statistics say nothing of the personal sacrifices and human suffering that lie behind them. What can you do to protect yourself against the high cost of long-term care? The answers are only partial ones and will continue to be so until we as a nation establish a comprehensive long-term health-care program. In the meantime, in addition to advocating that your legislators support such a program, you need to plan ahead to safeguard yourself against catastrophic health-care costs.

IT DOESN'T LOOK SO BAD IN THE BROCHURE.
THEY GOT SHUFFLEBOARD....

Develop a Medicaid plan

If you need nursing-home care, chances are that either you or Medicaid will foot the bill. Don't count on Medicare because its nursing-home benefit is extremely limited. And don't pin your hopes on private long-term-care insurance. While such policies have improved over time, good ones are still hard to come by and then may be prohibitively expensive. Veterans Administration benefits? Don't expect much: The nursing-home coverage is limited and generally won't last longer than six months. That leaves you and Medicaid, and by the time Medicaid starts paying, you've already paid—and paid dearly.

Obviously, unless you've planned ahead, you or your spouse can wind up virtually broke.

Obviously, unless you've planned ahead, you or your spouse can wind up virtually broke. So-called divestment planning is often used when one person wants to qualify for Medicaid nursing-home benefits as quickly as possible while preserving life savings. Typically, middle-income persons benefit most from divestment or Medicaid planning; people with very low incomes will quickly qualify for Medicaid if they need nursing-home care, while the more affluent can afford to pay the nursing-home tab.

One caveat to divestment planning is that it may help qualify you or a loved one for substandard nursing-home care. It's sad but true that the quality of nursing-home care provided to Medicaid residents is lower than that provided to private-pay patients. Consequently, most people prefer not to have to go in Medicaid. But if avoiding Medicaid is not an option for you, divestment planning is worth considering.

I'll briefly discuss some of the most common divestment-planning strategies to familiarize you with your options. You should, however, seek professional financial planning and legal advice before you jump in as there are many variables that can come into play in specific cases.

Hold assets in exempt form

As I mentioned earlier, Medicaid applicants can keep certain assets (including their home and car) and still qualify for benefits. They can also legally use nonexempt assets, such as money in a savings account or CD, to buy exempt assets. This way, instead of paying the nursing home all of their savings, they've invested in their home, car, and household goods. So pay off your mortgage and fix up your car!

Transfer assets thirty months or more before a nursing-home stay

One way to increase the likelihood of qualifying for Medicaid nursing-home benefits is to give a portion of your spouses assets to you, your siblings, other relatives, or friends. If you do this at least thirty months before entering a nursing home, the transferred assets will not be counted in determining Medicaid eligibility. (If a person disposes of assets for less than fair market value within thirty months of a nursing-home stay, states can delay eligibility for Medicaid.)

Shuffle assets between spouses

Because a couple's combined life savings are counted in determining eligibility for Medicaid, this strategy will not help the nursing-home spouse qualify more quickly for benefits. However, it may help preserve the couple's assets if the spouse living at home dies first.

Seek a court order

One way for a spouse at home to retain more assets and income than state law normally allows is to seek a court order authorizing the additional support.

"The court order can go so far as to award her all of the community and even her husband's separate property. Whatever property the court order allocates to her need not be spent for her husband's nursing home costs, and there is no limit on the amount that the court can award her. Similarly the court order can require the husband to pay her spousal support even if it exceeds [the Medicaid limit], and even if it comes from his Social Security or pension [benefits]," according to Marc Hankin, in Fulbright & Jaworski's Elder Law Newsletter.

People whose income and assets are fairly modest, however, should not buy long-term-care policies.

SET UP A TRUST SIXTY MONTHS OR MORE BEFORE ENTERING A NURSING-HOME

When you establish a trust, you transfer ownership of certain property and other assets to a trustee, who agrees to manage the resources according to the terms of the trust document. New rules have made it more difficult to establish a trust so that its assets will not be counted in determining Medicaid eligibility. But it's not impossible, provided you get legal and/or financial planning advice.

BUY A LONG-TERM-CARE INSURANCE POLICY

Another method for protecting yourself against the high cost of long-term care is to buy private long-term-care insurance, which typically covers nursing-home stays and some home-health services. People whose income and assets are fairly modest, however, should not buy long-term-care policies. They would quickly qualify for Medicaid benefits should they need to stay in a nursing home. There are other issues involved in this strategy, including what is and isn't covered, to what extent, and the conditions under which a specific thing may be covered. Often times policies are set up to look good on paper, but have stipulations as to the conditions and circumstances of the coverage.

To identify a good long-term-care policy, *Consumer Reports* tells shoppers to look for one that:

- pays $135 (in 2000) for each day the policyholder is in a nursing home (most long-term-care policies are

indemnity policies which pay a fixed benefit per day rather than a percentage of actual charges);
- begins paying benefits at least twenty days after the policyholder enters the nursing home;
- offers four years' worth of coverage for each nursing-home stay;
- provides benefits for unlimited days for all stays;
- pays full benefits for care provided in skilled, intermediate, and custodial-care facilities;
- does not have a requirement for a prior hospital stay;
- covers home care without requiring previous nursing-home or hospital confinements;
- specifically covers patients with Alzheimer's disease;
- includes a waiver of premium feature that allows policyholders to stop paying premiums once they're confined to a nursing home;
- is guaranteed renewable for life;
- is offered by a reputable company.

ATTACH A LONG-TERM-CARE RIDER TO A LIFE INSURANCE POLICY

This arrangement allows all or a portion of the policy's death benefit to be prepaid in monthly installments to a living policyholder should he or she enter a nursing home. Long-term-care riders can cost as little as $100 per year on a $100,000 universal policy. ("Stand-alone" long-term-care insurance policies may cost ten times that amount.) There are several caveats involved, such as tax issues and the common practice of bundling different types of insurance into one package, which frequently results in purchasing coverage that you do not need. As with virtually every option, consult an experienced professional before buying.

JOIN A CONTINUING-CARE RETIREMENT COMMUNITY

Many consider continuing-care retirement communities (CCRCs) as the ultimate in retirement living. Many CCRCs offer guaranteed health care for the resident's lifetime. Costs (very expensive) and services vary from community to community, so shop around and get as much information as possible before making your decision.

AND THEY GOT A DOCTOR RIGHT THERE WATCHING YOU PLAY HORSESHOES...IN CASE YOU RING SOMEONE'S NECK ON ACCOUNT OF YOUR FAILING EYESIGHT, I SUPPOSE....

Cutting Insurance Costs: Dos and Don'ts

What you should do:

- Shop around for the best policy. Benefits, premiums and restrictions vary widely. The best deals aren't always offered by the insurance giants such as Blue Cross and Blue Shield. Lesser known companies may offer comparable (and sometimes better) coverage for lower rates.

- Take advantage of free-look provisions, which allow you time to examine the policy with the option of returning it for a refund if you're not satisfied.

- Complain to your state department of insurance if you believe you've been misled by an insurance agent or advertisement. In some cases, these regulatory offices can negotiate a refund.

- Review insurance policies annually to make sure they still fit your situation. Some policies, such as hospital-indemnity and most long-term-care policies, pay benefits in fixed amounts and may be outdistanced by inflation. Consider whether the policy should be updated or dropped.

- Familiarize yourself with changes in Medicare benefits and legislation affecting health-care insurance. Newspapers and your local Social Security office are good sources of information.

- Ask insurance agents for their business cards. Not only may you need to contact them again, but you should know with whom you're dealing.

What you shouldn't do:

- Don't buy a policy without first asking for, and then scrutinizing, the disclosure statement describing its costs, benefits, and restrictions.

- Don't buy insurance that duplicates benefits you receive under another policy. It's a waste of money.

- Don't replace a policy just because it's out of date. Switching may subject you to new exclusions (conditions that the policy won't cover) or waiting periods (the time until benefit payments begin). If possible, add new benefits to the old policy.

- Don't keep a policy just because you've had it for a long time. If it doesn't provide the coverage you need, drop it.

- Don't lie on insurance applications. If you don't mention that you have diabetes or a heart condition, you may not get paid when you need the money.

Money-Saving Tips

- If you pay your own premiums directly, try to arrange to pay them on an annual or quarterly basis. It's cheaper than month-to-month because you can earn interest on the money between payment periods.

- Review all insurance bills and reimbursements. It happens—a company bills you for a service you never received or fails to reimburse you for a service you paid for out of pocket. If you have questions about a bill or payment, get answers! Contact your insurer, or if you have a group plan, your group administrator.

- Exercise your right to appeal Medicare decisions. The appeals process takes time, but it is often worth the effort if Medicare completely denies your claim or pays only a small fraction of it. Appeals procedures are described in *The Medicare Handbook.* For more help filing an appeal, call your local senior center or Area Agency on Aging for a referral to a Medicare advocacy program.

- Buy generic drugs. Despite some clear-cut variations in product quality, they're generally as safe and effective as brand-name medicines, and cheaper by as much as 40 to 50 percent. Your pharmacist can tell you which drugs are available in generic form and can answer your questions about them. Your pharmacist can also tell you which ones have been approved by the Food and Drug Administration (FDA) as being identical to the brand-name product.

- Get a second opinion whenever you have any questions about a recommendation for treatment or surgery, especially major surgery. Try to find a well-known expert who is not closely affiliated with the doctor making the recommendation; a second opinion is valuable only if it's independent.

- Exercise regularly, watch your diet, and get adequate rest. If you smoke, quit. A dollar's worth of prevention saves about $9 worth of cure.

Health insurance is a product you buy with the hope that you'll rarely have to use it. Should you need medical care, however, one of the last things you'll want to worry about is how to cover the expense. The best strategy for avoiding such a dilemma is to insure yourself adequately, not by purchasing a fistful of health-care policies, but by buying only the right policies—those that fit your personal needs.

The Ballad of Bill and Betty Continues…

The best strategy for avoiding an insurance dilemma is to insure yourself adequately, not by purchasing a fistful of healthcare policies, but by buying only the right policies—those that fit your personal needs.

When Betty was diagnosed with a minor but chronic lung disease that required expensive medication for the rest of her life, they were shocked to learn that one of the government programs like Medicare or Medicaid wouldn't pay for it. They ended up joining an HMO in their area—more out of reaction to not being eligible for any government healthcare programs than out of any thoughtful planning. They buy generic brands of most of the drugs Betty needs. While this saves them some money, the monthly drug bills are still considerable.

Now Bill's back is acting up. Some days it's so stiff he can't get out of bed. Long a nagging ailment, he has never sought treatment for it. You see, Bill is the type who won't seek medical attention until he's at death's door. Betty says she was attracted to him when they were younger because he was the strong, silent type. Now she thinks—and tells him often—that her strong and silent man has turned into a silent and stupid man. She says it, of course, with the unmistakable glint of genuine love and affection in her eyes.

The Boomers' have begun to see the writing on the wall. They're not getting any younger. Even if Bill's back problem isn't serious, it's likely that, like most aging folks, they will have more and more medical expenses in the years to come.

CHAPTER NINE

THE 10 BIGGEST MISTAKES RETIREES MAKE

Planning for your retirement is not rocket science. It is, however, a very technical "art" that requires a thorough knowledge and understanding of the latest rules and regulations, trends and legislation. It also requires an objective, disciplined approach that steers clear of emotional advice and sentimental decision-making. Failing that, there are a whole host of mistakes that can be—and often are—made when planning for retirement. In this chapter I'll discuss the 10 biggest mistakes that I routinely see—mistakes that, with the advice and guidance of an experienced retirement planner, can be easily avoided.

Another nice mess you've gotten me into.

—Stan Laurel

1. LISTENING TO THE WRONG PEOPLE

Too often retirees get tips and advice from friends and relatives and other well-intentioned but frequently only vaguely informed sources.

Promise, large promise, is the soul of an advertisement.

—Samuel Johnson

One of my pet peeves is articles from magazines and other periodicals that are primarily concerned with selling the publication rather than sound financial advice. I'm reminded of the "fad diets" that are frequently trumpeted on the cover of diet and weight loss magazines: "Eat Everything You Want and Lose 25 Pounds In One Month!" or "The Dessert Diet: Lose Weight and Eat All the Cheesecake You Want!"

As improbable as these claims may seem, they sell magazines—and lots of them. Unfortunately, retirement and financial planning publications are not above the same type of sensationalism. "10 Easy Steps to Becoming a Millionaire!" or "Make a Million Dollars in Two Weeks!"

Another common suspicious source of advice is the know-it-all brother-in-law. You know the type: he has the most up-to-date information on every subject under the sun, and is never at a loss to offer it up—though he never seems to remember were he heard it or read it or saw it. You wouldn't take his advice on what brand of outdoor paint to use on your house. Why would you take his advice on planning your retirement?

And don't forget about your neighbor's son the accountant—the boy-genius and wonderful son who's called every Mother's and Father's Day since he left home: "Oh, he knows everything there is to know about the stock market! We put him through Wharton and now he handles all our money! He knows all about this day-trading stuff and the commodities market! He was employee of the month last month at his brokerage firm!"

If he's such a financial genius and wonderful son, why are his parents still living in the cramped bungalow where he grew up and not in their dream home on the lake?

My point is that everyone you ask will have an opinion or know someone who knows exactly what you should do. It's human nature to want to make oneself appear informed and helpful. And indeed, anecdotal stories of someone else's personal experience may serve a useful purpose in that they can often add a perspective to your thought processes on a particular subject or issue that you might not have considered before. "When Janey was a baby, she wouldn't eat strained carrots. She used to get the most horrible look on her face and turn red every time I fed them to her. The doctor said I shouldn't worry too much about it, and that I should try strained peas instead."

Unfortunately, the retirement and financial planning landscape is quite a bit more complex than flavors of strained baby food, and anecdotal/experiential information from friends and relatives is almost never the most enlightened information available. And like Janey's reaction to strained carrots, one particular retirement strategy may not be the best for you. In fact, I can almost guarantee that it won't. With some exceptions, each and every individual has a different set of circumstances in both their financial situation and their retirement goals. Important factors like timing (When did your best friend talk to a professional planner? Two years ago? Three years ago? If the same person I advised three years ago came to me today, my advice would almost certainly be different. New laws, different interest rates, new qualifying requirements, etc.) and goals (What did your best friend want out of their retirement strategy? Dream home? Vacation condo? Or simply a comfortable standard of living?) are specific to any strategy and key in determining what course should be taken.

So before you listen to arbitrary voices and drop half your life-savings on the hottest tech stock that your neighbor's wonderful Wharton grad mentions in his yearly Mother's Day phone call home, consult an experienced retirement planner on what will work best for you.

2. GETTING CAUGHT BY THE NEW 20 PERCENT WITHHOLDING PENALTY FOR LUMP-SUM DISTRIBUTIONS

Every day unsuspecting (and uninformed) retirees get caught by some new rule or regulation or law or legislation passed by Congress to catch retirement-aged people who, quite simply, make too much money. With the ever-increasing pressure to make Social Security work and create a more "egalitarian" economic system, laws get passed every year that have the effect of reneging on previous policies and practices. Unfortunately, many retirees fall victim to this particular brand of social economic reform. The most recent example of this is the 20 percent withholding penalty for lump-sum distribution.

If you are retiring or transferring a lump-sum distribution from a company plan at a later time and you don't follow the paperwork rules exactly right, you could end up having 20 percent of your money withheld from your distribution. To make matters worse, you can end up paying taxes and penalties if you can't make up this 20 percent difference out of your own pocket.

For example, if you were getting a $200,000 distribution earmarked for an IRA but didn't fill out the necessary paperwork correctly, you could have $40,000 withheld from your transfer. And if you didn't have the $40,000 to put into the IRA to make up for the withholding, you would be taxed on that $40,000 even though you never got the money. You could end up paying as much as $16,000 in taxes, depending upon your bracket. Furthermore, if you are under 59 and 1/2 years old and this happens to you, you have to pay an extra 10 percent penalty on top of all the extra taxes.

So before you go willy-nilly into the financial jungle, discuss the issue of traps, pitfalls and hidden doors with an experienced retirement planner.

3. Choosing the Wrong Pension Option

Suppose you were about to retire. Your spouse didn't work and so had no pension coming in. You are given a choice of several retirement options from your company, with a confusing range of choices of how to handle the pension pay out should you die before your spouse. You decide to take the higher pay out now, counting on your life insurance to cover your spouse if you die. If you die in a tragic accident months after your retirement, your spouse is left with no pension income. Only the proceeds from your life insurance policy. In many cases, within a few short years, your spouse will have to go to work just to make ends meet.

The mistake here is not having someone prepare a detailed financial projection of which option would best meet their needs—before making an irrevocable decision. I've seen this scenario too many times to call it an aberration. Of course there are some cases wherein the higher pay out option is best. Again, no two cases are exactly alike. As always, check with an experienced planner to help you figure out what type of a retirement pay out is best for your situation.

4. Misunderstanding What Medicare and Medicaid Do and Don't Pay For

If I had a dime for every time I heard "I thought Medicare would cover my medical expenses," I wouldn't have to worry about my own retirement planning because I would be wealthy.

Medicare does cover certain medical expenses after you pay the deductible. Many of the medical expenses that aren't covered by Medicare are usually covered by a Medicare Supplement policy. However these supplements still do not cover extended nursing home care. (Medicare pays for up to 100 days of skilled care. On day 101, you could find yourself in big financial trouble as nursing home care can run upwards of $3,500 per month.)

All too often, retirees are unaware of what expense Medicare and Social Security cover—and there are a lot that they don't. An unplanned for situation like the necessity of long-term nursing home care can literally wipe out a family financially. Obviously, no responsible retirement planning is complete without knowing what is and isn't covered by government-sponsored and private health care plans.

There's every indication that health care coverage issues will be poked and prodded endlessly over the next few years. It has become a primary area of concern for politicians and their reelection hopes, so it's likely that what is and isn't covered will change on the whim of whatever position gets them reelected. Now more than ever, it's imperative that you seek the guidance of someone who knows what is happening and what is likely to happen in the future.

5. Not Understanding the Tax Rules for IRAs, Pensions, Income, Etc.

All too often, retirees are unaware of what expenses Medicare and Social Security cover—and there are a lot that they don't.

How much should you withdraw from your plans? When should you withdraw? Or should you let the money sit and use other money to live and pay bills? Should you take a withdrawal from your IRA to pay off your car so you'll have lower monthly payments? Should you stop working at a certain time to collect Social Security now? Perhaps you should wait to apply? Or should you decide to work part-time, how will it affect your Social Security payments? What about the taxes on your Social Security income? Are there legal and safe ways to reduce it? What about the taxes on the interest on your CDs? Is there a better way to invest to reduce those taxes? And on and on and on!

There are hundreds of tax decisions you need to make—many of which you probably have no idea that they even exist! One of the biggest (and most frequent) mistakes I see is retirees who pursue a financial strategy with little or no knowledge or understanding of the tax rules and regulations. It's absolutely futile to jump into the treacherous financial waters without making sure your income, estate and gift taxes are as low as legally possible. I've had clients who have saved $200, $300 and even as much as $500 a month in taxes simply by knowing the laws and how to legally reduce their taxes. Any retirement planner who's worth his or her salt can help you with the seemingly infinite number of tax rules and regulations, and the best ways to maximize your position.

6. NOT KNOWING HOW INFLATION DESTROYS YOUR MONEY, AND NOT TAKING ACTIONS TO PREVENT IT FROM LEAVING YOU BROKE

Two things you must understand about inflation:

1) It's here to stay;
2) If you don't plan properly and set yourself up to handle the decrease in the value of your money, there's a good chance you'll end up broke.

There are hundreds of tax decisions you need to make—many of which you probably have no idea that they even exist!

There are a number of factors involved in inflation, not the least of which is the incredibly inefficient way our government has handled our economic situation. The long and short of it is that we end up paying higher taxes, the cost of living grows ever more expensive, the cost of medical care grows ever more expensive, and we pay higher prices for goods and services. At the current level (2-3 percent, if you believe the government's statistics), costs will double in 24 years. In the 70s when we had a 12 percent inflation rate, costs doubled in six years. Lest we forget the lessons of the past, our economic problems in the 70s were the result of the shortage of domestic oil and high cost of foreign oil, high interest rates, and a shortage of cheap labor. Sound familiar?

There's every economic indication that inflation as we knew it in the 70s will be making a comeback—and soon. Which means that now is the time to seek out hedges against it; not once you've purchased a fortune's worth of bonds or T-bills. Once again, an insightful financial planner can help you.

I THOUGHT THEY DISCOVERED A CURE FOR INFLATION BACK IN THE 70S....

Inflation is the one form of taxation that can be imposed without legislation.

—Milton Friedman

7. THINKING "RISK" ONLY INVOLVES LOSING PRINCIPAL

There's more risk in risk-less investments than you think. Most notably, there's the risk of lost purchasing power (inflation working against CDs, bonds, etc.—the concept of negative real rate of return). What you need to do is figure out how much monthly income you need, then build a plan that uses the tax favored items to assure you get the cash flow you need, and avoid wasting money on the taxes you don't need, with assets that have some chance to keep up with inflation.

8. PAYING FOR THE WRONG KINDS AND WRONG AMOUNTS OF INSURANCE

There's little wonder that many retirees make this mistake. The insurance landscape is one of the most convoluted

Too often retirees are easy marks for agents hustling to make quotas and win the trip to Hawaii.

and confusing areas of retirement planning. Many times a recent retiree will hang on to old insurance just because they've had it for a long time and don't like change. Also, many retirees make emotional decisions when it comes to insurance. Too often retirees are easy marks for agents hustling to make quotas and win the trip to Hawaii. It's very difficult for a beloved spouse to cut corners here—especially when the beneficiary is setting in the next chair. Objectivity in such an emotional subject area is always difficult. Help with decisions regarding insurance may be the most important area to have a professional planner help you with.

9. PLANNING FOR YOUR RETIREMENT WHEN YOU ARE ALREADY RETIRED

One of the most common—and costly—mistakes you can make is waiting too long to start planning. Sometimes it happens suddenly—an unexpected layoff late in your career, or opting for a "sweet" early retirement program from a company trying to shrink its payrolls. Most often, however, it's simply a matter of procrastination. In the back of your mind, you know that you have a pension waiting for you, so you never really give much thought to planning your retirement. Too often, people make the mistake of thinking that a pension means you've already done their retirement planning. Not so. In any well-conceived retirement strategy, a pension should be merely a small part of the overall plan—a reliable source of cash if you choose pay out over time.

While it's never too late to do the right thing, the right time to plan for your retirement is long before the happy day comes. Otherwise, it just could be that the day you've been looking forward to all your life may not be so happy.

10. Not Doing Consistent, Careful, Ongoing Planning

Most soon-to-be retirees approach retirement planning as a "wing-it-as-you-go" proposition. You've got your investments, your insurance, all the elements of a retirement strategy. Now you let it ride. Unfortunately, to get the most out of your strategy, you need to monitor the performance of your strategy, make adjustments whenever necessary, or stay the course when you realize your conscientious planning is paying off.

The reason this is absolutely necessary is that the rules and regulations change, interest rates change, the financial possibilities change. The kind and quality of the financial tools available to you are in a constant state of fluctuation. To put it in a different perspective, think of your retirement plan or strategy as a computer and its operating system. Now think of the various options available in your retirement strategy as software programs that you load onto your computer and operating system. Every month—probably every week—new programs are introduced and updates for existing programs are developed. These programs are designed to get the most out of your computer's capabilities and your own skill and imagination. They make it possible for you to achieve your goals more easily and effectively.

Obviously there are far too many developments in the financial tools available to you for you to keep up with all of them. Chances are you'll only hear about major ones that get air time on the evening news. Ideally, you'll want to have someone that knows and understands all the developments as frequently even small adjustments in policy can effect your portfolio and mean substantial savings or earnings if it's incorporated into your existing strategy. This is where an experienced financial planner who's on top of the latest developments can be invaluable, and I

The kind and quality of the financial tools available to you are in a constant state of fluctuation.

strongly recommend that you find a good one that you're comfortable with—even if it's just in a consultant capacity. The information and advice he or she can bring to the table could mean the difference between a so-so retirement strategy and a dynamic strategy that works for you as it should.

The Ballad of Bill and Betty Boomer Continues…

Life had always seemed to work out well for Bill and Betty. When problems or difficulties came up, they handled them. Simple as that. And then they went on about their business. They'd never had to plan very much; it always seemed like life made their plans for them. When Bill, Jr. came along unexpectedly, they made a few plans that actually seemed to have already been made for them. The same for Nellie. Life, to them, seemed to be something that revealed itself as they went along. And they were happy to live that way.

Now all of the sudden, Bill was approaching retirement age and they didn't have a plan. What's more, a plan didn't seem to be revealing itself to them. In the back of their minds, they knew—even years ago—that they would have to give some thought to their retirement. Still, that day seemed to be far away in the future. Now, all of the sudden, it's upon them. With retirement upon them, and despite a whole host of recent situations that should have sent financial planning warning flags up, they still hadn't made any plans.

CHAPTER TEN

WHAT TO LOOK FOR IN A FINANCIAL PLANNER

Early to bed and early to rise, makes a man healthy, wealthy and wise.

—Benjamin Franklin

Perhaps by now you may be wondering whether or not you should consider working with an advisor. If that's the case, the following questions may be useful in helping you decide.

1) Have I accumulated enough to live for the rest of my life without working?

2) Will I be as financially secure ten or twenty years from now as I am today if I incur long-term care needs?

3) If I retire early should I file for Social Security early at a reduced rate?

4) I can't risk losing money. Should I avoid investments that are not guaranteed like stocks or mutual funds?

5) Are stocks and mutual funds good retirement investments?

6) Am I receiving the highest possible returns with the lowest risk?

7) Are my taxes as low as they can be?

8) Will your estate avoid taxes, probate, future spouses, Medicaid spend down and ex-in-laws?

Most people really don't know what questions to ask, or what things they should be aware of.

9) Is there a way to avoid or reduce taxes on my Social Security benefits?

10) Do I know how much I should withdraw from my IRA/401(k)?

If your answer to any of the above was "no" or "I don't know," you could probably benefit from working with a good qualified advisor. However not all financial advisors are the same. Most people really don't know what questions to ask, or what things they should be aware of. When it comes to your money, you had better know! Picking the right advisor can help you and picking the wrong one can be a big mistake.

In today's fast-paced economy where the rules and opportunities change almost daily, you cannot afford to take chances. If you're like most of us, you're probably always looking for a deal or something for nothing. But when it comes to something as important as your retirement, a good advisor can be the best investment decision you'll ever make.

WHAT DO YOU MEAN HE "LOOKED" LIKE HE KNEW WHAT HE WAS DOING!?

Many people are as insecure when it comes to hiring a financial advisor as they are hiring a lawyer or interior decorator.

Many people are as insecure when it comes to hiring a financial advisor as they are hiring a lawyer or interior decorator. The feeling that, as soon as you enlist their services, it's all going to begin to spiral out of control is a genuine and honest reaction—and not always unfounded.

To help ease your anxieties about consulting a financial advisor, I've developed a list of ten areas that will help you feel more on top of everything.

1) ASK FOR FIVE REFERENCES

Three should come from current clients, and two from other professionals like accountants or bankers.

There are three reasons why I suggest getting references from professionals. First, any person in business should have at least three satisfied clients. Consequently, client references alone may not be enough. Second, if a planner cannot produce two other professionals that will attest to his ability as a financial planner, he may not be respected by his peers. Finally, outside professionals in the community see all kinds of things and will usually be aware of what kind of advice is available and of the quality of services provided.

2) ASK IF THEY CHARGE FEES FOR THEIR SERVICE

No one works for free! If they're not charging a fee, they must be making money from sales of products. If they're making 100% of their income from product sales, they must sell enough to make up for the people who did not buy. If there is a price to be paid, it must be paid by either the planner or by you. Which one do you think it will be?

Buying financial products without a plan is like having surgery without an exam.

3) IF THEY DON'T CHARGE FEES, ASK THEM HOW YOU CAN BE SURE THAT THE ADVICE THEY WILL PROVIDE IS IN YOUR BEST INTERESTS

Make them tell you how they analyze a situation, and what process they go through to arrive at recommendations.

What you want to hear is that they first find out how you feel about your money and finances. Then they will get a detailed understanding of your income, assets, debts, company benefits, etc. Finally, you want to hear that they will work up an action plan that addresses all of your concerns, and that gives you choices—choices of the different ways your concerns can be handled, and with the pros and cons of each method.

This process allows you the ability to make decisions from an educated basis instead of from salesmanship. There is nothing wrong with being sold financial products as long as they fit your needs, and not necessarily those of the sales people.

4) IF A PLANNER SELLS PRODUCTS, ASK IF THE PRODUCTS CAN BE OBTAINED IF NO PLAN IS PREPARED

The best plans are the ones that are developed as a result of an in-depth interview.

Buying financial products without a plan is like having surgery without an exam. Call me crazy, but I sure wouldn't want a doctor operating on me until he knew what was wrong with me. Doctors should pass their exams before operating.

The same holds true for a financial planner who sells product without an analysis. If you take away the planning process, you are left with nothing more than a product salesman. A plan can be many things. It may be a short one-pager, all the way up to a thick set of graphs and charts. Neither is necessarily better than the other. However, even if the plan is short, the interview process should not be. The best plans are the ones that are developed as a result of an in-depth interview. The planner must ask about all of your issues. Not just the ones he/she can make money on. They should ask about any and everything you are concerned with, including taxes, education funding, home financing, company benefits, insurance, estate planning, retirement goals and investments. A good planner knows how to get to know you, your goals, your fears. If you find, after the interview process, that he/she understands your financial situation and your emotional nature, then you are probably with a good planner.

5) IF THERE IS A FEE, DO NOT PAY MORE THAN FIFTY PERCENT OF THE FEE IN ADVANCE

Although a retainer is often requested, most professionals do not require one hundred percent of their fee in advance. Paying the balance upon completion of the plan assures you that the job will be finished to your satisfaction.

6) ASK ABOUT THE PLANNER'S FINANCIAL BACKGROUND

As a rule, if you have a significant amount of wealth, consider only planners that have been providing financial services for at least five to ten years. Although there may be some very good planners with less experience, why take the chance. I was once an inexperienced planner. I got my experience working with people who were also just starting out. Select an advisor who has more financial experience than you do.

7) SEEK ONLY THOSE PROFESSIONALS THAT HAVE RECOGNIZED FINANCIAL DESIGNATIONS

Education is an important ingredient in selecting a financial advisor. An educated financial advisor should have at least one of the following credentials:

- CRPC-Chartered Retirement Planning Counselor
- CEA-Certified Estate Advisor
- CFP—Certified Financial Planner
- ChFC—Chartered Financial Consultant
- CLU—Chartered Life Underwriter
- APFS—Accredited Personal Financial Specialist

- o Admission to the Registry of Financial Planning Practitioners

The above organizations require that you pass an initial exam and obtain continuing professional education. By seeking a planner with one or more of the above designations, you can be assured that the planner has made a commitment to obtain sufficient knowledge to excel in financial planning.

Make sure you feel you will be getting excellent service and advice, and won't be treated as a number.

8) THE BENEFITS YOU RECEIVE MUST EXCEED THE COST OF THE PLANNING

Otherwise, what's the point. If you spend more for planning advice than you are likely to receive in increased revenue, there's no benefit and, indeed, there may very well be negative benefits beyond the obvious loss in revenue, such as lost time spent talking to planners.

9) ASK THEM HOW THEY KEEP UP ON THE CONSTANTLY CHANGING FINANCIAL ENVIRONMENT

Do they get research from their parent company? Do they attend workshops or go to classes? Are they studying for an advanced degree? Do they subscribe to financial publications other than general media (trade journals as opposed to *Newsweek* or the *Wall Street Journal*)? This is important since good planning consists of having the most current, accurate information available.

Ninety-four percent of all Americans will not be able to retire on the same standard of living they had before they retired.

10) Ask the planner how many clients they have and how many new ones they take on

It is impossible for anyone to handle thousands of clients with a high level of personal service. Make sure you feel you will be getting excellent service and advice, and won't be treated as a number. It's true that every planner can handle a different client load. It depends on their personality, staff, resources, outside professionals, etc. Be sure to find out how they get things done and how fast they can respond to your needs. Of course these are sometimes hard questions to ask; no one wants to feel like they're insulting a potential friend and business associate. But keep in mind that it's your money on the line!

Some other things that you want to be conscious of when you're looking for a planner include:

Integrity

Does the firm build a plan based upon realistic assumptions? Does the firm tell you what you want to hear or what you need to hear? Do you like and trust the firm's advisors and staff?

Competency

Is the firm reputable? Do you know of others who have had favorable experiences?

Specialization

Does the firm specialize in retirement transistion? Is the firm familiar with your employer's retirement plan and procedures?

Support Staff

Is there always someone available to answer your questions? Does the firm have the staff to carefully monitor your account?

Getting the right help is critical to your success. According to the Social Security Administration, 94 percent of all Americans will not be able to retire on the same standard of living they had before they retired. Why do you suppose such is the case? My experience tells me that it's because most people spend more time planning their next vacation than they do planning their family finances.

Most people are fastidious planners of their vacations—when they'll leave, what needs to be done before they leave, what to bring, how to get to the airport, what to do when they get there, how they will get around once they get there, where they'll eat, and on and on, down to how much money they'll allocate for souvenirs. Are you that thorough with your personal finances?

It takes a lot of time and knowledge to analyze and plan your money. Raising a family can be as much of a full-time job as a full-time job itself. There's little time left to study tax laws and other financial information. Consequently, planning your finances often gets delayed until a "more convenient" time.

If you remember nothing else in this book, remember that, quite simply, you must plan for the future today because the future will become the present whether you plan for it or not. Failing to plan can mean wasting thousands of dollars in overpaid taxes, earning an after tax rate of return that is lower than inflation, suffering a lower standard of living at retirement, losing as much as 55 percent of your estate to estate taxes and, quite simply, not achieving your financial goals in life.

Proper planning is your best chance to beat the odds and join the six percent that are successful. Take any one hundred people at the start of their working careers and ask them how many believe they will be financially independent. I would be terribly surprised if even one person answered "not me!"

Life well spent is long.

—Leonardo da Vinci

However, according to the Social Security Administration, 40 years later one will be wealthy, five will be financially secure, five will continue working, 36 will be dead, and 54 will be dependent upon their Social Security checks, relatives, friends or even charity for a minimum standard of living.

Planning is the major difference between the six percent that were successful and the 94 percent that failed to accomplish their objectives. I'm not saying that planning will make everything run perfectly and smoothly for the rest of your life, but I can tell you from experience that it will significantly improve the possibility of that happening.

Best wishes for the best of your life.

The Ballad of Bill and Betty Boomer Continues….

Faced with the likely possibility of increasing medical expenses, a precarious current financial situation, and all the stress, confusion and uncertainty that comes with the territory, Bill and Betty decide to consult a professional financial planner. Though it was not Bill's nature—or Betty's, for that matter—to turn personal responsibility over to someone else, they decided that the peace of mind—not to mention the money they would save in taxes and other areas that the planner was helping them with—was worth it.

EPILOGUE

The Ballad of Bill and Betty Boomer Continues...

"That's four out of seven this week," Betty said with a satisfied look and big grin.

"I'm challenging yesterday's ruling," Bill replied.

Bill and Betty had been betting on the exact minute the sun would rise above the eastern range. Last spring they were able to build their dream home in the mountains. The financial planner they hired had organized their finances and managed to put them on a budget whereby they could accomplish their financial and life goals. Now every morning they sit on their wrap-around porch and bet on sunrise. So far, Bill owes Betty three homemade gourmet dinners, a week of running her bubble bath, and a puppy.

As for their children, Bill, Jr. is working for a non-profit organization that drafts public initiatives that empower consumers. On weekends he volunteers at a local homeless shelter. Nellie, after getting her M.B.A., married a mergers and acquisitions attorney in a big, wonderful old fashioned wedding. She has an adorable 18 month-old little girl named Lauren, and she and her husband are in the process of adopting a two year-old little boy from Romania. Vice-president of new market development for a multi-national software company, she works half-time in her home office and half-time in her downtown high rise.

For their 40th anniversary, Bill, Jr. and Nellie sent their parents to Europe for a whole month. When they returned, Bill, Jr. had just put the finishing touches on a wrap-around porch on his parents' new log cabin in the mountains, and Nellie had furnished the entire house with custom made log furniture.

"I'll go double or nothing on tomorrow," Betty said as she returned to the porch with two fresh cups of coffee.

"If things keep going the way they're going, I'll be cooking you gourmet dinners and running you bubble baths for the rest of our lives," Bill replied.

"Now you know my master plan," Betty said with a sly but heartfelt grin.

AFTERWORD

So you've given some serious thought to your financial situation. Now what?

It's always a good time to take action on a thing when the the thing is fresh on your mind. If you've taken the time to fill out the worksheets in previous chapters, much of your legwork is already done. If such is the case, getting the ball rolling on your retirement planning strategy is as easy as picking up the phone or sending an email. With the information that you've compiled from this book, virtually every planner in the business can get to work on your retirement strategy. Indeed, we'd be happy to get the ball rolling for you ourselves. To contact Townsend and Associates:

Townsend and Associates, Inc.
11178 N. Huron, #5
Northglenn, CO 80234
(303) 452-5986
jtownsend@myplanningpartner.com
www.myplanningpartner.com.

RESOURCES

Books, Magazines, Articles and Brochures

Avoiding the Medicaid Trap: How to Beat the Catastrophic Costs of Nursing-Home Care, by Armond D. Budish. New York: Henry Holt, 1989.

Baby Boomers, by Paul Light. New York: W.W. Norton & Co.

Encyclopedia of Financial Gerontology, Lois A. Vitt and Jurg K. Siegenthaler, eds. Westport, CT: Greenwood Press.

Forbes Magazine: Forbes Inc., 60 Fifth Ave., New York, NY 10011. (800) 888-9896. Biweekly; $57 per year.

Gifting to People You Love: The Complete Guide to Making Gifts, Bequests, and Investments for Children, by Adriane G. Berg. New York: Newmarket Press, 1996.

How to Protect Your Life Savings from Catastrophic Illness and Nursing Homes, by Harley Gordon. Boston: Financial Strategies Press, 1994.

Investor Beware: How to Protect Your Money from Wall Street's Dirty Tricks, by John Lawrence Allen. New York: John Wiley & Sons, 1993.

Kiplinger's Personal Finance Magazine: 1729 H Street, NW, Washington, DC 20006. (800) 544-0155. Monthly; $19.95 per year.

Kiplinger's Retire and Thrive: Remarkable People Share Their Creative, Productive and Profitable Retirement Strategies, by Robert K. Ottenbourg. Washington, DC: Kiplinger Press, 1995.

Lifetrends, by Jerry Gerber, Janet Wolff, Walter Klores, and Gene Brown. New York: Macmillan Publishing Company.

Make Your Own Living Trust, by Denis Clifford. Berkeley, CA: Nolo Press, 1993.

Managing Your Health Care Financing, by Susan Polniaszek. Available for a nominal charge from the United Seniors Health Cooperative, 1334 G Street, NW, 5th Floor, Washington, DC 20005. Tel.: (202) 393-6222.

Medicare Handbook, The, by U.S. Department of Health and Human Services, Health Care Financing Administration. To obtain a free copy, visit your local social security office or call toll-free (800) 234-5755.

Medicare Made Easy, by Charles B. Inlander and Charles K. McKay. Reading, MA: Addison-Wesley, 1988.

Money Magazine: P.O. Box 60001, Tampa, FL 33660. (800) 541-1000. Monthly (13 issues); $39.95.

Our Aging Society: Paradox and Promise, Edited by Alan Pifer and Lydia Bronte. New York: W.W. Norton & Co.

Plan Your Estate, by Clifford Denis. Berkeley, CA: Nolo Press, 1992.

Simple Will Book: How To Prepare a Legally Valid Will, 2nd Ed., by Clifford Denis. Berkeley, CA Nolo Press, 1995.

Social Security, Medicare and Pensions, 6th Ed., by Joseph L. Matthews. CA: Nolo Press, 1996.

Statistical Record of Older Americans, edited by Arsen J. Darnay. Detroit: Gale Research Inc.

Taking Your Money Out: IRAs, 401(k)s and Other Retirement Plans, by Twila Slesnick and John C. Suttle (Nolo, $21.95); not exactly light reading, but an excellent starting point.

This Aging Society, by William C. Cockerham. Upper Saddle River, NJ: Prentice Hall.

Tomorrow's Choices: Preparing Now for Future Legal, Financial, and Health Care Decisions (D13479), and *Health Care Powers of Attorney* (D13895): AARP Fulfillment, 601 E. Street, NW, Washington, DC 20049; (800) 424-3410.

Long Term Care: A Dollar and Sense Guide, by the United Seniors Health Cooperative. Washington, DC, 1994. (1331 H Street, NW, Washington, DC 20005; (202) 393-6222.

Your Pension: Things You Should Know About Your Pension Plan (brochure). Pension Benefit Guarantee Corp., 2020 K Street, NW, Washington, DC 20006.

Websites

www.brill.com Interactive mutual fund information.

www.irs.gov/prod/cover.html Internal Revenue Service.

www.insure.com Insurance News Network.

www.irajunction.com A fledgling site offered by mPower, which also runs another top investor website called 401kafe.com.

www.irahelp.com Sponsored by C.P.A. and IRA newsletter publisher Ed Slott, the chief attraction is a forum where he'll help answer your IRA questions.

www.investools.com Independent investment and financial information.

www.mfmag.com Mutual funds information from *Mutual Funds Magazine*.

www.ssa.gov Social Security on line.

www.townsendassoc.com My own firm's website.

Associations and Organizations

Health Insurance Association of America
1001 Pennsylvania Avenue, NW
Washington, DC 20004-2599
(800) 942-4242

Medicaid (Medi-Cal in California)
For more information about eligibility and benefits, contact the state department that administers Medicaid, sometimes called the department of public social services, human services, welfare, or health. Check the government section of your telephone book.

National Association of Insurance Commissioners
120 West 12th Street, Suite 1100
Kansas City, MO 64105.
Tel.: (816) 842-3600.

National Council on Aging
409 3rd Street, SW
Suite 200
Washington, DC 20024
(202) 479-1200.

Social Security Administration
Visit a local office for information about Medicare or call toll-free: (800) 234-5755.

State Department of Insurance
Check the government section of your phone book for the address and telephone number.

SEC (Securities and Exchange Commission)
Office of Consumer Affairs
450 Fifth Street, NW, Room 2111
Mail Stop 2-6
Washington, DC 20549
Telephone: (202) 272-7440; (202) 272-7065 (telecommunications for the deaf) Free brochures.

REFERENCES

Allen, John Lawrence. 1993. *Investor Beware: How to Protect Your Money from Wall Street's Dirty Tricks.* New York: John Wiley & Sons.

Berg, Adriane G. 1996. *Gifting to People You Love: The Complete Guide to Making Gifts, Bequests, and Investments for Children*. New York: Newmarket Press.

Budish, Armond D. 1989. *Avoiding the Medicaid Trap: How to Beat the Catastrophic Costs of Nursing-Home Care*. New York: Henry Holt.

"Beyond Medicare." *Consumer Reports*, June 1989: 375-391.

Clifford, Denis. 1993. *Make Your Own Living Trust.* Berkeley, CA: Nolo Press.

Clifford, Denis. 1992. *Plan Your Estate.* Berkeley, CA: Nolo Press.

Clifford, Denis. 1995. *Simple Will Book: How To Prepare a Legally Valid Will,* 2nd Ed. Berkeley, CA: Nolo Press.

Cockerham, William C. *This Aging Society*. Upper Saddle River, NJ: Prentice Hall.

Darnay, Arsan J., ed. *Statistical Record of Older Americans.* Detroit: Gale Research Inc.

Gerber, Jerry, Janet Wolff, Walter Klores, and Gene Brown. *Lifetrends*New York: Macmillan Publishing Company.

Gordon, Harley. 1994. *How to Protect Your Life Savings from Catastrophic Illness and Nursing Homes.* Boston: Financial Strategies Press.

Inlander, Charles B., and Charles K. McKay. 1998. *Medicare Made Easy.* Reading, MA: Addison-Wesley.

Light, Paul. *Baby Boomers.* New York: W.W. Norton & Co.

Matthews, Joseph L. 1996. *Social Security, Medicare and Pensions*, 6th Ed. Berkeley, CA: Nolo Press.

Ottenbourg, Robert K. 1995. *Kiplinger's Retire and Thrive: Remarkable People Share Their Creative, Productive and Profitable Retirement Strategies.* Washington, DC: Kiplinger Press.

Pifer, Alan and Lydia Bronte, eds. *Our Aging Society: Paradox and Promise*. New York: W.W. Norton & Co.

Slesnick, Twila and John C. Suttle. *Taking Your Money Out: IRAs, 401(k)s and Other Retirement Plans*. Berkeley, CA: Nolo Press.

Vitt, Lois A., and Jurg K. Siegenthaler, eds. *Encyclopedia of Financial Gerontology.* Westport, CT: Greenwood Press.

INDEX